T0381109

# *Love Notes*

***Send forth your light and truth***

PATTY CLARK

WestBow Press books may be ordered through booksellers or by contacting:

WestBow Press
A Division of Thomas Nelson & Zondervan
1663 Liberty Drive
Bloomington, IN 47403
www.westbowpress.com
1 (866) 928-1240



ISBN: 978-1-9736-8477-0 (sc)
ISBN: 978-1-9736-8476-3 (e)

Print information available on the last page.

WestBow Press rev. date: 05/07/2020

# WEEK ONE

MONDAY

## *Life's Purpose*

*And he made from one man every nation of mankind*
*to live on all the face of the earth, having determined*
*allotted periods and the boundaries of their dwelling place,*
*that they should seek God,*
*and perhaps feel their way toward him and find him.*
*Yet he is actually not far from each one of us.*

Acts 17:26-27

We often get confused about the *true* purpose of life, but…God created us to know, love and enjoy Him now and forever. That is, without a doubt, the most important fact of life. And really that one all important "fact" is the key to living the abundant life Jesus died to give us…the "key" to living the way He intended and wants us to live. Life can be so simple when we look at it through God's eyes.

*Deep within us all there is an amazing inner sanctuary of the soul,*
*a holy place, a Divine Center, a speaking Voice,*
*calling us home. – Thomas Kelly*

## WEEK ONE

TUESDAY

*You shall love the* L*ORD* *your God with all your heart*
*and with all your soul and with all your might.*

Deuteronomy 6:5

Jesus blessed us with the gift of life so that we could know and love Him. Period! End of Story. Our problem is that we get so wrapped up in ourselves and fixated on earning money so we can buy lots of things…we leave Jesus out of the equation entirely. That's the reason we get confused and so overwhelmed.

Jesus' has a beautifully simple plan for our lives. He wants to have a personal and intimate relationship with us and be our Ever Present Closest Friend. Life is, really, about receiving His love and loving Him in return.

## WEEK ONE

WEDNESDAY *Life's Purpose*

*Then I looked, and I heard the voice of many angels,*
*numbering myriads of myriads and thousands of thousands,*
*saying with a loud voice,*
*'Worthy is the Lamb who was slain,*
*to receive power and wealth and wisdom and might*
*and honor and glory and blessing!'*

Revelation 5:11-12

God gives life. He saves our souls from hell and, on top of all that, He walks with us through the good, the bad and even the ugly. He deserves our thanksgiving and praise! He planned our inception, formed us in our mother's womb, scheduled the day of our birth and volunteered to die for our sin so we could live the best possible life. He is worthy of honor and glory! He wants to take care of us and, really, He is the only one who can.

## WEEK ONE

THURSDAY 

*The Spirit himself bears witness with our spirit*
*that we are children of God, and if children, then heirs—*
*heirs of God and fellow heirs with Christ, provided*
*we suffer with him in order that we may also be glorified with him.*

Romans 8:16-17

---

When we believe in Jesus Christ and we accept Him as our personal Savior, that's when we inherit the free gift of eternal life. We have heaven to look forward to not hell. Just think about it! When we die we get to spend eternity with Jesus. As awesome as that sounds…there's more. When we accept Jesus as our Savior we not only become *"new creations,"* we also become *"joint heirs"* of everything that belongs to Him. All the love, joy, peace, knowledge, and power that He possesses…He places all that good stuff at our disposal so we can live life as He intended and do the good work He equipped and ordained us to do. It's all so amazing. Left to our own devices, being the frail people we are, we can't do much of value on our own. But with Jesus… we can change the world.

## WEEK ONE

FRIDAY

*I am the true vine, and my Father is the vinedresser.*
*Every branch in me that does not bear fruit he takes away,*
*and every branch that does bear fruit he*
*prunes, that it may bear more fruit.*
*Already you are clean because of the word*
*that I have spoken to you.*
*Abide in me, and I in you. As the branch*
*cannot bear fruit by itself,*
*unless it abides in the vine, neither can you, unless you abide in me.*
*I am the vine; you are the branches. Whoever*
*abides in me and I in him,*
*he it is that bears much fruit, for apart*
*from me you can do nothing.*

John 15:1-5

---

Staying close to Jesus is the most important thing in life. It's also *the* greatest challenge we face as Christians. We live in a crazy and mixed up world. There are so many distractions and things to do. Life can be overwhelming and often feels like it's spinning out of control. But that's where Jesus comes in. He is always with us and at our side. Just thinking about Him can bring peace to our tormented and weary souls. Whispering His name helps focus our attention on the things of heaven and strengthens our hearts.

We're only human. But God is GOD! *"Nothing is impossible with Him."* (Luke 1:37)

## WEEK ONE

SATURDAY/SUNDAY *Life's Purpose*

| Facts of Life |
| --- |
| -Life is about knowing God. |
| -Life is about loving God and being loved by Him. |
| -We are joint-heirs with Christ. |
| -Abiding in His presence is life's greatest joy. |

Personal Reflections:

# WEEK TWO

MONDAY

## *Facts of Life*

*I will set my eyes on them for good,*
*and I will bring them back to this land.*
*I will build them up, and not tear them down;*
*I will plant them, and not pluck them up.*
*I will give them a heart to know that I am the* LORD,
*and they shall be my people and I will be their God,*
*for they shall return to me with their whole heart.*

Jeremiah 24:6-7

This promise from God provides us with a glimpse into our heavenly Father's heart. He loves us and wants to bless us. And He will…if we let Him. It's hard to imagine just how much God loves us. It's unfathomable, really. Even before we were born He wanted us and had a personalized and specific plan for each of our lives. He didn't *have* to create us; no one forced Him to. He made us because He *wanted* us. And He wanted us so He could have a relationship with us. He loves us *that* much. It's utterly incomprehensible. And all He asks in return is our love.

## WEEK TWO

TUESDAY *Facts of Life*

*Have this mind among yourselves, which is yours in Christ Jesus,*
*who, though he was in the form of God,*
*did not count equality with God a thing to be grasped,*
*but emptied himself, by taking the form of a servant,*
*being born in the likeness of men. And*
*being found in human form,*
*he humbled himself by becoming obedient to the point of death,*
*even death on a cross.*

Philippians 2:5-8

---

Jesus came to earth and became a slave for *our* sake, not His own. He didn't *fight* for His rights the way we do. He gave His rights away, voluntarily. He humbled Himself and died for *our* sin. That's love. Think about it! He thought more about us than He did Himself. Amazing. We wouldn't even be here having this conversation right now if it weren't for Him

Pride, arrogance and an exaggerated sense of self-importance can get in the way of our loving the way Jesus loves. Humility and giving our lives away is a good place to start.

# WEEK TWO

WEDNESDAY *Facts of Life*

*This is my commandment,*
*that you love one another as I have loved you.*

John 15:12

---

"Love one another." It sounds so simple, even easy, but we know it's not. That's because we're human, willful and self-centered. Left to our own devices it would be impossible for us to love the way Jesus loves. But we can do that very thing with His help. It's all about letting Him love others unconditionally through us.

Loving God's way is a learned phenomenon. It will take a lifetime of practice and a whole lot of God's grace for us to get it right.

## WEEK TWO

THURSDAY *Facts of Life*

*Do nothing from selfish ambition or conceit,*
*but in humility count others more significant than yourselves.*
*Let each of you look not only to his own interests,*
*but also to the interests of others.*

Philippians 2:3-4

---

Jesus is with us, all the time, watching over us. He wants our success even more than we do. What we must come to grips with is the reality that being selfish doesn't work. Selflessness is the key to loving the way Jesus loves and truly enjoying a life that pleases Him. That doesn't come naturally. We're human, sinners and self-centered by virtue of our fallen nature. Unfortunately self-centeredness is part of the human condition. But God expects more from us and will enable us to be more like Him. That's because He cares, and we're supposed to care about others. We *can* do that, right? It's all about doing life His way and honoring Him.

FRIDAY

*Facts of Life*

I Corinthians 13:4-13

I Corinthians 13 is called the "Love Chapter." These sacred verses can be a bit intimidating when you read it for the first time. But in spite of the fact that we may *not* love the way Jesus loves right now…at this moment in time…Paul is telling us that we can learn. There's hope for us you see and we're not stuck where we are.

We learned to walk by walking. We learned to run by running. We can learn to love others by following Jesus' example and loving others the way He first loved us. No! Loving others isn't always easy. But we can reach our goal by taking one God-honoring baby step at a time.

SATURDAY/SUNDAY



## Facts of Life

-God created me for relationship.

-Loving God with all my heart is the most important thing.

-I can learn how to love the way Jesus loves.

Personal Reflections:

# WEEK THREE

MONDAY

*Speech*

*Let the words of my mouth and the meditation of my heart be acceptable in your sight, O LORD, my rock and my redeemer.*

Psalm 19:14

---

What *should* I say, Lord? Have you ever stopped to think how much sweeter our relationships with one another might be if we got into the habit of asking Jesus that simple question before we said anything? Just a slight pause in a conversation can make all the difference in the world. It's like that old adage about counting to ten before speaking. A few seconds gives us a chance to *think*, get our emotions under control before we blurt out something that, perhaps, shouldn't be said.

Inviting Jesus to play an active and ongoing part in all our conversations…is it all that surprising that things are bound to improve if that's the direction we decide to go?

# WEEK THREE

TUESDAY

*My Speech*

*I will ponder all your work,*
*and meditate on your mighty deeds.*

Psalm 77:12

---

Instead of gossiping, complaining and nattering on and on about things that don't matter…why wouldn't we practice silence, at least until we had something good to say? God is listening. Don't you think He'd rather we build each other up instead of tearing one another down? Wouldn't the world be a better place if we stopped arguing and made an effort to get along?

There's an amazing positive progression that takes place in the human spirit when we focus our attention on pleasing God. Our focus shifts. Our attitude is dramatically altered. And, really, it takes very little to have a positive influence in our little corner of the world.

## WEEK THREE

WEDNESDAY *My Speech*

Whoever would love life
and see good days
must keep their tongue from evil
and their lips from deceitful speech.

I Peter 3:10 (NIV)

---

Have you ever blurted something out in the heat of the moment and afterwards wished you hadn't said what you said? Of course you have. Everyone has. The good news is we can learn to control our tongues and do things differently with God's help from this point on. The truth contained in this verse is powerful. Our lives in general and relationships with others will go way better and be sweeter when we do. Besides – who says we have to have the last word on any given matter or, even, have something to say about everything all the time?

# WEEK THREE

THURSDAY *My Speech*

*These are the things that you shall do:*
*speak the truth to one another;*
*render in your gates judgments*
*that are true and make for peace.*

Zechariah 8:16

---

What would the world be like if all we spoke out loud was God's truth instead of gossip, complaints and lies? Jesus never lied, about anything. He chose to say nothing from time to time… when He was falsely accused of crimes He didn't commit and tried in court for an example. He remained silent, but He didn't argue or lie. And when He did speak…He spoke words of truth… words that would encourage, comfort, guide and help people find ways to honor Jehovah and thrive.

We can do the same thing. We start by studying His Word and He promised that His Spirit would teach us everything we need to know when we do.

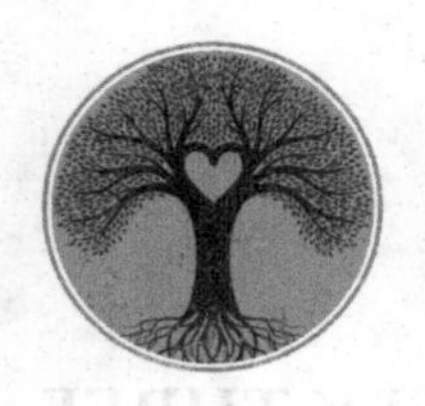

## WEEK THREE

FRIDAY

*My Speech*

Ephesians 4:17-24

*Therefore, if anyone is in Christ, he is a new creation. The old has passed away; behold, the new has come II Corinthians 5:17.*

The way we used to think, talk and behave...meeting Jesus face to face and surrendering our lives to Him changes things. We've been blessed with a second chance to live life the right way...His way...and we have to remember that. Think of it as the ultimate kind of do-over...an opportunity to live lives of purity, spiritual excellence and love and serve God. We may not understand how all that happens but the good news is, now, we get to tell others about what all the good stuff Jesus has done.

## WEEK THREE

SATURDAY/SUNDAY *My Speech*

### Facts of Life

-The Words that come out of our mouths should please God.

-All of God's Word is true.

-What other people say is important.

Personal Reflections:

# WEEK FOUR

MONDAY

## *Kindness Matters*

*He has told you, O man, what is good;*
*and what does the LORD require of you*
*but to do justice, and to love kindness,*
*and to walk humbly with your God?*

Micah 6:8

---

*"Act justly." "Be kind." "Walk humbly with your God."* Micha's words are incredibly powerful, especially today in the twenty first century. There's so much injustice, meanness and arrogance running rampant in our world. Maybe that's why Jesus said, *"Treat others the way you want to be treated."* We're supposed to listen to God, obey God and abandon our misplaced preoccupation with ourselves and what's going on in this world. That is extremely important since imitating the world is what got us into the mess we're in in the first place.

## WEEK FOUR

TUESDAY

*Kindness Matters*

*For God so loved the world, that he gave his only Son,*
*that whoever believes in him*
*should not perish but have eternal life.*

John 3:16

Love is a powerful force. So is kindness. God loved us so He sent His Son to die for our sin. That's love! Jesus did for us what we could not do for ourselves, died on a cross so we could be saved from spending eternity in hell. *That's kindness.* Obviously we can't do exactly what Jesus did. That is beyond us. But we *can* do something. We can help a neighbor carry groceries from their car into their home. We can smile at a waitress who seems to be having a bad day. We can make something special for dinner or write a note of encouragement and tell someone that they are valuable and we appreciate them. We all have something to offer.

## WEEK FOUR

WEDNESDAY *Kindness Matters*

*Let not steadfast love and faithfulness forsake you;*
*bind them around your neck;*
*write them on the tablet of your heart.*

Proverbs 3:3

There are times when we can be mean as human beings, hateful and even nasty. Or…we can be kind. We have a choice in this matter. What's it going to be? What will *you* do? Think about it. Instead of complaining about how awful the world is…you could make a difference. You could be part of the solution that may just change our world. Everyone can change the way they treat others. We can all make a concerted effort to change our family dynamic, alter the emotional climate of our marriage and inspire loyalty and a strong sense of responsibility amongst coworkers. Besides - doing what is right and good is contagious. Jesus gave what He had to give. We can do the same thing. In fact, we're supposed to.

# WEEK FOUR

THURSDAY *Kindness Matters*

*But love your enemies, and do good, and lend,*
*expecting nothing in return, and your reward will be great,*
*and you will be sons of the Most High,*
*for he is kind to the ungrateful and the evil.*

Luke 6:35

---

"Love your enemies." That's not exactly the "norm" in our world. If someone says or does something bad to us…more often than not we want to retaliate. It's the way of the world. It's part of our fallen human nature. It's not what God wants. But it *is* what we do.

Jesus is different. He is kind, even to the evil and ungrateful. He thinks more about others than He does Himself. And after all He's done for us…shouldn't we at least try to follow in His footsteps? He deserves to receive glory, honor and praise.

FRIDAY

## *Kindness Matters*

*Be kind to one another, tenderhearted,*
*forgiving one another, as God in Christ forgave you.*

Ephesians 4:32

---

*Do unto others as you would have them do unto you.* It is such a simple thing and profound truth. The quality of life for all humanity would improve dramatically if we were genuinely interested more in others than we are ourselves.

We live in a world that is filled with people who are lost, confused, hurting and lonely. Surely we can come along side each other, demonstrate random acts of kindness and give something of ourselves away. Plus, being kind to others improves our own disposition and attitude from the inside out. Have you ever thought about that?

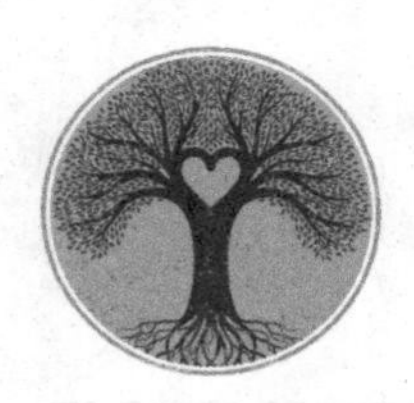

## WEEK FOUR

SATURDAY/SUNDAY *Kindness Matters*

### Facts of Life

-My loving and being Kind is important to Jesus.

-Jesus cares about me. I should care about others.

-I will become more like Jesus as I spend time with Him.

Personal Reflections:

# WEEK FIVE

MONDAY

*For while we were still weak, at the right time Christ died for the ungodly. For one will scarcely die for a righteous person—though perhaps for a good person one would dare even to die—but God shows his love for us in that while we were still sinners, Christ died for us.*

Romans 5:6-8 (NIV)

---

Problems happen. It goes with the territory of being human and the ongoing process of living life. The biggest "problem" we face as human beings is sin. Adam and Eve rebelled against God in the Garden of Eden. We inherited their sin and predisposition to rebel. We couldn't do anything about it, but Jesus did for us what we could not do for ourselves. He died on a cross and paid the price for our sin. Placing our faith in Jesus insures that our sins are forgiven and we will live for all eternity in heaven with Him. Sure. We will still have problems. And yes. We will still have to face some trials. The good news is - Jesus will be with us, all the time and the battles belong to Him.

## WEEK FIVE

TUESDAY

*God is our refuge and strength,*
*a very present help in trouble.*

Psalm 46:1

There is nothing to be afraid of. Why? Because God is God! He's on His throne and in control of everything. Absolutely! The world *can* be a scary place. But God is watching over us. He cares and is on our side.

We can spend our entire lives running away from God. But why would we? We can live self-sufficient lives and separate ourselves from Him. But why would we? The Almighty God of the Universe…the One who made us and died to save us…He wants to love us, teach us, bless us and guide our every step. In a divinely magical way…as we abide in His presence, Jesus replaces darkness with light, despair with hope and our sorrow with peace and joy. Nothing is impossible with Him.

## WEEK FIVE

WEDNESDAY

*Draw near to God, and he will draw near to you.*
*Cleanse your hands, you sinners, and purify your hearts,*
*you double-minded.*

James 4:8

---

We don't have to "do" anything on our own. In fact we're not supposed to. God is with us, all the time, every day. He gave us the gift of life and wants to be involved in everything we say, think and do.

It's humbling when you finally come to grips with the fact that the great big God of the Universe is madly in love with you and wants to be involved in your life, during the good times and the bad, when we're in trouble and when we are celebrating a victory. When we draw near to Him He promises to draw nearer to us. A subtle shift in our thinking is all that is required.

## WEEK FIVE

THURSDAY 

*Rejoice in the Lord always; again I will say, rejoice.*
*Let your reasonableness be known to everyone.*
*The Lord is at hand; do not be anxious about anything,*
*but in everything by prayer and supplication with thanksgiving*
*let your requests be made known to God.*

Philippians 4:4-8

---

We worry. It just comes naturally to human beings, unfortunately. And it is an easy and dangerous trap to fall into. There are no benefits or rewards in worrying. Anxiety takes our attention off of God and refocuses it onto the things of this world, circumstances and ourselves. It can rob us of joy, peace and accomplishes nothing positive and is a big fat waste of time.

But we don't have to worry. We can turn to Jesus and fix our attention on Him instead. He loves us and has a solution to every problem and will provide us with whatever is required. The good ol' hymn: *Turn Your Eyes On Jesus* comes to mind.

# WEEK FIVE

FRIDAY

## *Weathering the Storms*

Psalm 25:16-22

*Turn to me and be grace to me,*
*for I am lonely and afflicted.*
*The troubles of my heart are enlarged;*
*bring me out of my distresses.*
*Look upon my affliction and my trouble, and forgive all my sins.*
*Look upon my enemies, for they are many,*
*and they hate me with violent hatred.*
*Guard my soul and deliver me; do not let me be ashamed,*
*for I take refuge in You.*
*Let integrity and uprightness preserve me,*
*for I wait on You.*
*Redeem Israel, O God,*
*out of all this trouble.*

## WEEK FIVE

SATURDAY/SUNDAY *Weathering the Storms*

### Facts of Life

-God is on our side.

-God genuinely cares for us.

-God will help us if we let Him.

Personal Reflections:

# WEEK SIX

MONDAY

Malachi 3:6-10

God wants to bless us. He always has. This extraordinary passage in Malachi makes that perfectly clear. Jesus said that He died to give us "abundant" life. He doesn't want anyone to do without anything that is good for them. The key of course is to live life the way He intended it to be lived. That requires absolute surrender.

The Lord God doesn't change. That's why Malachi's words are so important. He wants for us today in the twenty first century what He wanted for His people in Old Testament times. He created us for relationship. The blessings we instinctively long for can only be found in Him.

## WEEK SIX

TUESDAY

*Give, and it will be given to you. Good measure,*
*pressed down, shaken together,*
*running over, will be put into your lap.*
*For with the measure you use it will be measured back to you.*

Luke 6:38

God gladly shares all that He is and all that He has with us. Contrary to popular opinion life isn't about money, popularity, fortune and fame. It's about knowing God intimately and giving away to others what we receive from Him. Our humble existence takes on a whole new and deeper meaning and energy and purpose when we care about God and others instead of being self-absorbed.

The Bible says, to not *merely look out for our own personal interests, but also for the interests of others* (Philippians 2:3-4). The fine art of being *others oriented* is a spiritual art that *can* be learned.

# WEEK SIX

WEDNESDAY

Exodus 19

A "treasured possession." It's hard to imagine that, being the flawed and imperfect creatures we are, that God still holds us in high regard. It's hard to understand why. But He wanted us and made us and died for our sin so we could know, love and be loved by Him. Then He sent His Spirit to live *in* us so we could experience and enjoy an abundant life. How can we *not* be humbled by such extravagance?

When you think about the multiplicity of ways God has already blessed us: given us eyes to see, ears to hear, hearts that beat, hands that create and noses that can smell…isn't it fitting and right to bless Him with our gratitude?

## WEEK SIX

THURSDAY

*Blessed are those whose strength is in you,*
*in whose heart are the highways to Zion.*

Psalm 84:5

The word *"blessed"* means: to be favored by God. When we give up and surrender our lives to Jesus…He gives us His best. When we stop focusing on ourselves and spend time in His presence… that's how we learn the truth about who Jesus is and are blessed. That's why He created us in the first place, so we could seek after Him and know and love Him with all our heart.

Life can be pretty simple if we do it God's way. And when we do? He favors us for doing what is right.

## WEEK SIX

FRIDAY

*His divine power has granted to us all things that pertain to life and godliness, through the knowledge of him who called us to his own glory and excellence, by which he has granted to us his precious and very great promises, so that through them you may become partakers of the divine nature, having escaped from the corruption that is in the world because of sinful desire.*

II Peter 1:2-4

---

Believing in Jesus and surrendering our lives to Him is the precursor to having everything we need to achieve our divine potential, spiritually excel and change the world. It is because of His divine power working in us that we are forgiven. It is because of the free gift of salvation that we are delivered from hell. It is because of the Holy Spirit living in us that we have the divine strength we need to resist temptation, rise above our humanness and become courageous and effective ambassadors for Jesus Christ.

Because of Jesus we can move mountains and bring Him glory. That's the most important thing.

## WEEK SIX

SATURDAY/SUNDAY

### Facts of Life

-God wants to bless us.

-God will finish the work He started in us.

-God will share everything He has with us.

Personal Reflections:

# WEEK SEVEN

MONDAY

*Anger*

*Refrain from anger, and forsake wrath!*
*Fret not yourself; it tends only to evil.*

Psalm 37:8

Getting angry serves no positive purpose, at all. It doesn't do any good. It only does harm. But we get mad anyway. For a lot of us it is a natural reaction to life. The worst thing is…it doesn't take much to set us off. The good news is life doesn't have to get the better of us. There's a better, safer and healthier way to live.

Anger isn't a sin in and of itself. It's what we *do* with anger that matters. Instead of letting anger send you into a tail spin…let it lead you into a closer and more intimate relationship with God. We can handle anything with God's help.

## WEEK SEVEN

TUESDAY

*Anger*

*Be angry and do not sin;*
*do not let the sun go down on your anger.*

Ephesians 4:26

---

We're all going to get angry from time to time. We're human. Unfortunately, getting upset is part of our fallen DNA. What's important to God is that when we *do* get mad we don't sin. We don't *let* our anger get the better of us, harm others or cause a seed of bitterness to grow deep within our souls. Satan works 24/7 to make sure that's exactly what happens. He works hard to ruin our lives and our relationship with Jesus. We can make sure all that bad stuff doesn't happen by being careful and alert, slow to speak and slow to anger. In that way our Savior wins and Satan loses.

## WEEK SEVEN

WEDNESDAY *Anger*

*Therefore I was provoked with that generation,*
*and said, 'They always go astray in their heart;*
*they have not known my ways.'*
*As I swore in my wrath,*
*'They shall not enter my rest.'*

Hebrews 3:10-11

God gets angry. Remember when He destroyed Sodom and Gomorrah and turned Lot's wife into a pillar of salt…or when He allowed His chosen people to be enslaved for 400 years by the Egyptians? The difference between God's anger and ours is His is righteous and just. For the most part, ours is not.

Getting mad and staying angry all the time isn't good for us. God knows that. It hurts Him when we treat each other badly and don't get along. God is love and we are supposed to love. We should celebrate and be humbled by the fact that He demonstrates extraordinary tolerance and restraint dealing with us.

# WEEK SEVEN

THURSDAY *Anger*

*Surely vexation kills the fool,*
*and jealousy slays the simple.*

Job 5:2

---

Anger destroys us from the inside out. It robs us of joy and peace, distorts our thinking, raises our blood pressure and can cause physical harm.

So when we do get mad why do we hang on to it and replay arguments and conversations over and over again in our minds? Why don't we pray, humble ourselves before God and let it go? The Lord wants to set us free from all that, and He will if we give Him a chance. He is always with us and willing to bless.

# WEEK SEVEN

FRIDAY *Anger*

*Give ear to my prayer, O God,*
*and hide not yourself from my plea for mercy!*
*Attend to me, and answer me;*
*I am restless in my complaint and I moan*
*because of the noise of the enemy,*
*because of the oppression of the wicked.*
*For they drop trouble upon me,*
*and in anger they bear a grudge against me.*

Psalm 55:1-3

---

Getting along with one another isn't always easy. In fact, sometimes, it can be just plain hard. King David knew all about relational difficulties. David was king. He also struggled with family problems, the crushing weight of responsibilities and relationships just like we do. But when his relationships were strained...his enemies were trying to kill him and was forced to hide out in a cave in fear for His life...David took refuge in God. He talked with God. He cried out to God and told the Almighty how he felt and asked for His help and got it. What God did for David He wants to do for us.

# WEEK SEVEN

SATURDAY/SUNDAY

## Facts of Life

-Anger serves no positive purpose.

-Anger is normal. It is what we do with it that makes the difference.

-When you get angry go to Jesus. He will help you work it out.

Personal Reflections:

# WEEK EIGHT

MONDAY *Obedience*

*Keep my statutes and do them;*
*I am the LORD who sanctifies you.*

Leviticus 20:8

---

Obedience is not an option as far as God is concerned. We may see it that way. He doesn't. Think about the rightness of obedience. We didn't exist. Then God made us and personally formed us in our mother's womb. Adam sinned. We inherited his sin nature and were destined to hell. Then Jesus died for our sin so we might be saved and live an abundant life. When we receive Him as our personal Savior He sends His Spirit to live in us, teaching us the true purpose of life and blessing us with the supernatural power to live a life that pleases Him. Of course we should obey Him! We owe Him everything.

## WEEK EIGHT

TUESDAY *Obedience*

*Only fear the* L*ORD* *and serve him faithfully with all your heart. For consider what great things he has done for you.*

I Samuel 12:24

---

We don't obey God because of what we can get from Him. We obey God because He owns us and He deserves nothing less. He blessed us with the most precious and extraordinary gift of life. What we do with that "gift" is up to us – our choice. Every single day we have to decide whether or not we're going to live for ourselves or Him, do what we want to do or dedicate our whole being to pursue the ambitions of His heart.

When you consider who God is...why wouldn't we obey Him?

## WEEK EIGHT

WEDNESDAY *Obedience*

*The end of the matter; all has been heard.*
*Fear God and keep his commandments,*
*for this is the whole duty of man.*

Ecclesiastes 12:13

Obedience is about trust and respect, really. We either care more about God than we do ourselves or vice a versa. Obedience isn't a matter of shaking in our boots and being terrified of God. It's a matter of demonstrating our love for God because He deserves to be loved.

He tells us how much He loves us in His Word. We prove how much we love Him by doing what He tells us to do. It makes perfect sense and gets easier one baby step at a time. The closer we walk with God the more we realize that obedience is the greatest form of worship.

## WEEK EIGHT

THURSDAY *Obedience*

*Now therefore mend your ways and your deeds,*
*and obey the voice of the LORD your God,*
*and the LORD will relent of the disaster*
*that he has pronounced against you.*

Jeremiah 26:13

---

We must pay the consequences of our actions, good or bad, whether we want to or not. The ugly reality is - We bring a lot of trouble on ourselves by the poor choices we make and by doing what is wrong. It's not what God wants or intended. That's why He gives us this warning in the Book of Jeremiah.

We were made to enjoy a personal relationship with Jesus. Being in right relationship with Him and living the way He would have us live assures us that we will be able to achieve our full potential and live an abundant life. Living in heaven for all eternity with Jesus, personal excellence, spiritual health and serving in God's church…that is what God intended for our lives.

## WEEK EIGHT

FRIDAY *Obedience*

*Why do you ask me about what is good?*
*There is only one who is good. If you would enter life,*
*keep the commandments.*

Matthew 19:17

---

We're all rebels at heart. We inherited Adam's rebellious heart unfortunately. The good news is we're not stuck where we are. God will help us…transform us…enable us by His divine power to live a different God-honoring life. The key is obedience.

When God says *"love one another,"* that's what we're supposed to do. When He tells us to forgive others the way we want to be forgiven, that's exactly what we have to do. When He commands us to seek after Him with all our heart and with all our soul and with all our might…well, you get the idea. God tells us how to live because He wants the best for us. He alone knows what is best for us. If we want to please God and spiritually succeed we must obey Him. We'd be fools not to.

## Obedience

### Facts of Life

-Life is about seeking and knowing God.

-God gave us the gift of life.

-Jesus is willing to lead us into life's best.

Personal Reflections:

# WEEK NINE

MONDAY *Word of God*

*The heavens declare the glory of God,*
*and the sky above proclaims his handiwork.*
*Day to day pours out speech,*
*and night to night reveals knowledge.*
*There is no speech, nor are there words,*
*whose voice is not heard.*

Psalm 19:1-3

---

God is speaking to us in and through nature all the time. He lifts the sun up every morning…lays it down in the west every evening. In the spring He creates a masterpiece of renewal and hope evident in every wildflower that pops its lovely head out of the sparkling translucent snow. He challenges us to clear the cobwebs out of our thinking and fill our minds with heavenly thoughts by studying His Word. He wants to teach us and grow us up to our full spiritual potential so we will be thoroughly engaged and excited about the living of life.

God is talking to us in a thousand ways. But the question is… are we listening?

## WEEK NINE

TUESDAY *Word of God*

*Blessed is the man*
*who walks not in the counsel of the wicked,*
*nor stands in the way of sinners,*
*nor sits in the seat of scoffers;*
*but his delight is in the law of the LORD,*
*and on his law he meditates day and night.*

Psalm 1:1-2

---

God planned for our success...before the beginning of time. His plan is perfect and, yes, even simple. He doesn't want us to live life the way the world does. He wants us to abide in Jesus, get to know Him intimately, do what He tells us to do and be like Him.

Jesus is the only one who can help us get all that done. Plus, He enjoys spending time with us. He wants to tell us the truth, reforming our twisted thinking and fill our spirits with what is healthy, true and right. All we have to do is seek Him, be still and listen. He has so many extraordinary things He wants to tell us.

# WEEK NINE

WEDNESDAY *Word of God*

Psalm 19:7-11

---

There is no down side to studying God's Word. The Bible is one hundred percent true. Everything God says in Scripture is "perfect," "trustworthy," "true" and "right". And in the scriptures we find everything we need to live a God-honoring life.

Why wouldn't we read the Bible if we're serious about living life to its fullest? Why wouldn't we want to spend time with the One who created the sun, moon and stars, the earth and all that is in it? Why wouldn't we sit at God's' feet and give Him a chance to reveal the "perfect" plan He has for our lives?

Think about that for a moment!

## The Word of God

*All Scripture is breathed out by God*
*and profitable for teaching,*
*for reproof, for correction,*
*and for training in righteousness.*

II Timothy 3:16

---

Everything we need to know about living life successfully is found in God's Word. No exceptions.

God didn't inspire and compile the Holy Scriptures because He didn't have anything else to do. He did it so we would be prepared and equipped to live an abundant life for His pleasure and glory. He wants us to succeed even more than we do. He loves us and cares deeply about our success and doesn't want us to stumble blindly and clueless through life. He tells us everything we need to know in His Word. All we have to read it.

# WEEK NINE

FRIDAY *Word of God*

*All Scripture is breathed out by God*
*and profitable for teaching,*
*for reproof, for correction,*
*and for training in righteousness.*

II Timothy 3:16

It isn't enough to listen to good preaching or attend Christian conferences, Bible studies or even Biblically based seminars. That's all good stuff, but God wants us to sit quietly at His feet and give Him a chance to speak divine truth into our lives. He has a whole lot He wants to tell us…teach us…so we can achieve our full potential and serve Him and love others in His name.

When we study God's Word His Spirit reveals Himself to us and fills us with divine courage and strength. Armed with these we can do anything.

# WEEK NINE

SATURDAY/SUNDAY *Word of God*

Facts of Life:

-God still speaks.

-Studying God's Word transforms our lives.

-Obedience is about loving Jesus.

Personal Reflections:

# WEEK TEN

MONDAY *Contentment*

*Better is a handful of quietness*
*than two hands full of toil and a striving after wind.*

Ecclesiastes 4:6

*Tranquility* is the absence of disturbance, tension and stress. And given the condition of our world, you wonder if true tranquility can be found on earth. Because of Jesus the answer is "Yes!" It is imperative to disengage every once in a while from our earthly existence and spend quality time with Him. Why? Because in Him we find peace, joy, refreshment for our souls and hope.

Jesus wants to make things better for us and He will if we slow down.

# WEEK TEN

TUESDAY

*Be still before the LORD and wait patiently for him;*
*fret not yourself over the one who prospers in his way,*
*over the man who carries out evil devices!*

Psalm 37:7

---

God's ways are not our ways. He tells us to *walk* through life not run...to *be still* so our hearts and minds can find rest, strength and renewal in Him. The truth is - We don't have to do all the things we do. Striving and struggling and fighting to make our own way through life, going, doing, producing and trying to make things happen for ourselves causes chaos and creates the most destructive and unhealthy kind of stress inside of us.

There is another way. The psalmist suggests that we should *"be still"* and "wait" upon the Lord. When we do He will lead and guide and bless. And that is how we grow up into the people He intended us to be.

# WEEK TEN

WEDNESDAY *Contentment*

*A glad heart makes a cheerful face,*
*but by sorrow of heart the spirit is crushed.*

Proverbs 15:13

A "glad heart." What does Jesus see when He watches over us? Something that makes him frown? Or something that makes Him smile? He doesn't want to see us work ourselves to death, running faster than we should and producing more than humanly possible. That's not what He created us for.

He made us so we could enjoy a personal relationship with Him. He longs to talk to us about so many things and teach us what is true, just and right. He longs for us to *be still* and commune with Him in prayer and include him in everything. That's what makes Him smile and makes for a glad heart.

## WEEK TEN

THURSDAY *Contentment*

*If we live by the Spirit, let us also keep in step with the Spirit. Let us not become conceited, provoking one another, envying one another.*

Galatians 5:25-26

---

Humbling ourselves and keeping in step with God's Spirit produces peace and contentment. When we resist and rebel against God, life becomes confusing and overwhelming, chaotic and there is always lack.

We pay an enormous price when we insist on doing our own thing and leaving God out of the equation. We find out what He wants us to do when we study His Word. We succeed and personally prosper when we admit we're not as smart as we thought we were and obey Him.

Peace - Walking in harmony with God's will is all that is required.

## WEEK TEN

FRIDAY

*Not that I am speaking of being in need,*
*for I have learned in whatever situation I am to be content.*

Philippians 4:10

---

Contentment is a learned phenomenon. Some people are born with it. I was not. Achieving contentment isn't easy, especially in the over active and tempting world we live in. Paul's life story should inspire and motivate us to at least try.

The apostle Paul was born into an affluent family and well educated. He held public office and served as a powerful and influential religious leader. He abused his power by persecuting the fledgling Christian church, even putting some members to death. Then Jesus met him on the Road to Damascus and saved him. From that point Paul's life dramatically changed. He planted Christian churches, preached the gospel, wrote over half the New Testament, was ship wrecked, held captive in a Roman prison for years at a time and…still in the Book of Philippians he boasts that no matter what he went through he learned to be content. And if he did…we can too.

## WEEK TEN

SATURDAY/SUNDAY

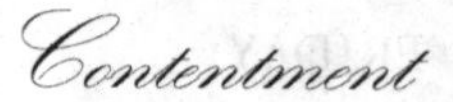

### Facts of Life:

-God's ways are not our ways.

-Drawing near to God produces contentment.

-Jesus is enough.

Personal Reflections:

# WEEK ELEVEN

MONDAY *Gratitude*

Psalm 100

God made us. We belong to Him. He saves our souls from hell so we can spend eternity in heaven with Him. He loves us and is with us all the time, in the good, the bad and even the ugly.

Gratitude is more than just a matter of positive thinking. Gratitude is a heartfelt response for Jesus choosing to be in our lives and extending His awesome life-changing love and mercy to us…getting involved and actively participating in each of our lives. Being humble and grateful changes our heart attitude. That's a given. We must choose to love on Jesus and thank Him for His generosity.

## WEEK ELEVEN

TUESDAY *Gratitude*

*Oh give thanks to the LORD, for he is good;*
*for his steadfast love endures forever!*

Psalm 118:1

God is good, and He loves us. He always has. He always will. His love is free, undeserved and unconditional; the best possible kind of love. His affections are limitless and exactly what the human spirit needs and instinctively craves.

We spend a great deal of our time, energy and attention trying to earn other people's acceptance, approval and love. Is it any wonder then why we're so frustrated and disappointed with life? Human relationships, as gratifying and important as they may be, cannot possibly provide us with what we were created for - To receive and return God's love and enjoy Him forever.

## WEEK ELEVEN

WEDNESDAY *Gratitude*

*Rejoice always, pray without ceasing,*
*give thanks in all circumstances;*
*for this is the will of God in Christ Jesus for you.*

I Thessalonians 5:16-18

---

What parent is not blessed by their child's thankful heart? God is our parent and feels the same way. The real challenge in this passage is the phrase *"give thanks in all circumstances."* It's easy to thank God when things are going good. But God wants us to thank Him even when life is challenging and hard.

I Thessalonians 5:16-18 is a command, not a request. Our Good Father is telling us to do something that may *seem* impossible. It's not. We must chose gratitude. We have to decide to thank God even when our circumstances are less than perfect. The process is easier when we focus on the Biblical fact that He promised He would work all things together for our good.

# WEEK ELEVEN

THURSDAY *Gratitude*

*Let there be no filthiness nor foolish talk nor crude joking, which are out of place, but instead let there be thanksgiving.*

Ephesians 5:4

We spend a lot of precious time talking about things that don't really matter...things that won't make any long term difference in anyone's life. The point is – Life's too precious to waste a whole lot of time.

Sure, we can complain about this, that and the other thing. Remember the Israelites? They grumbled about everything. But look where it got them. We have a chance to be different. Instead of complaining about everything, we can speak words of thanksgiving, happiness and genuine praise out loud instead. You and I can change our little corner of the world one word of gratitude at a time.

# WEEK ELEVEN

FRIDAY *Gratitude*

*Do not be anxious about anything,*
*but in everything by prayer and supplication*
*with thanksgiving let your requests be made known to God.*

Philippians 4:6

God doesn't want us to worry. Worrying accomplishes nothing and is a great big waste of time

Instead, our heavenly Father wants us to trust Him. He cares and is genuinely interested in our wellbeing and every detail of what's going on in our lives. We can talk to Him about anything… everything. In fact, scripture says that He sympathizes with our many weaknesses and is always "there" for us and willing to help. The bottom line in all of this is that God has a solution to every problem, an answer for every question and…nothing is impossible with Him.

# WEEK ELEVEN

SATURDAY/SUNDAY

## Gratitude

### Facts of Life:

-We belong to God.

-God loves us.

-We should be grateful and thank Him.

Personal Reflections:

# WEEK TWELVE

MONDAY *Peace*

*Agree with God, and be at peace;*
*thereby good will come to you.*
*Receive instruction from his mouth,*
*and lay up his words in your heart.*

Job 22:21-22

Peace of mind starts with being at peace with God. There can be no true peace in our lives apart from being in right relationship with Him. Surrendering our wills and putting ourselves under His authority…opening our hearts wide and receiving His love is essential to enjoying the peace we need and crave. God has a plan for our lives and knows what the future holds. We don't. He alone has the wisdom, knowledge and supernatural power that will enable us to reach our divine potential and become the people He created us to be. He leads. We follow. He directs. We obey. It's all so very simple, right?

# WEEK TWELVE

TUESDAY *Peace*

*May the* LORD *give strength to his people!*
*May the* LORD *bless his people with peace!*

Psalm 29:11

---

God is our peace and He wants to fill us with all the good things that can only be found in Him. We've all disappointed Him from time to time, but He goes on loving us. We've all made some awful life choices, but He doesn't give up on us. Instead, He tenaciously continues to conform us to the image of His Son and lead us into an abundant peace-filled life.

When we accept and settle into the comfort of His love we are blessed…blessed to overflowing so we can share with others the love and peace we received from Him.

# WEEK TWELVE

WEDNESDAY *Peace*

*Let me hear what God the LORD will speak,*
*for he will speak peace to his people, to his saints;*
*but let them not turn back to folly.*

Psalm 85:8

---

There are many voices screaming in this world and demanding our attention. But there is only one "voice" that can bring true peace to our souls, God's. He is our Father, our Creator, the lover and Savior of our souls. His Spirit lives in us and He only speak truth and wisdom into our lives, if we listen. He has already given to us everything we need to live a God-honoring life, love others the way He loves us and initiate and perpetuate positive change in the world for His glory.

We are precious to God and are valuable to Him. True and lasting peace is found when we cultivate intimacy with Him.

# WEEK TWELVE

THURSDAY

*Peace*

*You keep him in perfect peace*
*whose mind is stayed on you,*
*because he trusts in you.*

Isaiah 26:3

---

Controlling our thoughts isn't easy. Ideas…past conversations… problems and worries have a way of showing up uninvited in our minds and linger longer than we'd like them to. But there's a way to escape this self-destructive cycle.

The "way" is simple. We must set our mind on Jesus and the things of heaven, instead of the things of earth. Thinking about how much He loves us has a divinely magical way of calming the human spirit and encouraging our disappointed and overwhelmed hearts. Reflecting on the fact that God's supernatural power is at work in our lives wipes away doubt, fear, anxiety and renews our courage, strength and hope.

# WEEK TWELVE

FRIDAY *Peace*

*Peace I leave with you; my peace I give to you.*
*Not as the world gives do I give to you.*
*Let not your hearts be troubled, neither let them be afraid.*

John 14:27

Jesus is with us all the time. He never leaves us and He is bigger, smarter, stronger and more faithful than we can dream or imagine. There's no reason to be afraid of life when He is in control. And He *is* in control.

Make it your habit to read the bigger than life-stories in the Bible. They reveal God's love in magnificent terms and illustrate how able He is to handle anything. *Nothing is impossible with Him.* He created the earth and all that is in it. He made you and me. He delivered two million of His people from captivity…parted the Red Sea…healed the sick, gave sight to the blind and raised the dead. And what He did in Biblical times, He can still do. He will. Believe!

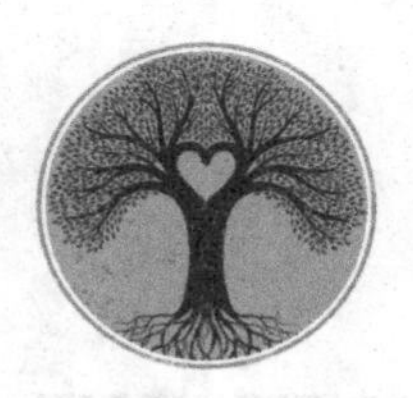

## WEEK TWELVE

SATURDAY/SUNDAY

**Facts of Life:**

-Peace is enjoyed by those who submit to God.

-God wants to be our peace.

-Keeping our minds stayed on Jesus wins the battle for our minds.

Personal Reflections:

# WEEK THIRTEEN

MONDAY

## *Bitterness*

*But I say, walk by the Spirit,*
*and you will not gratify the desires of the flesh.*
*For the desires of the flesh are against the Spirit,*
*and the desires of the Spirit are against the flesh,*
*for these are opposed to each other,*
*to keep you from doing the things you want to do.*

Galatians 5:16-17

Bitterness is a deadly disease. Left unchecked it infects the soul. If we aren't intentional in dealing with bitterness it can pervert our thinking, destroy relationships and contaminate every aspect of our lives.

This subtle and silent killer often takes root without our even knowing it. All it takes is for someone to disagree with our opinion…disappoint us…offer justifiable criticism that we take personally and brood over and we're doomed. We must be on the alert and aware and, most importantly, remember that God has a solution to our problem and will help.

## WEEK THIRTEEN

TUESDAY *Bitterness*

*Let all bitterness and wrath and anger and clamor and slander be put away from you, along with all malice.*

Ephesians 4:31

Jesus knows how difficult life can be. He lived on earth and has gone through everything. He faced temptation just like we do and, yet, He remained pure and without sin. On top of all that He knows us. He made us and understands how weak we can be. The good news is He's available 24/7. We can talk to Him any time, about anything. In fact He wants us to do that very thing.

Jesus never puts a "closed" sign on the door of His throne room or takes a lunch break or goes on vacation. He's interested in what's going on in our lives and cares deeply. He invites us to enter His presence and reason things out with Him. Now that is amazing, indeed.

# WEEK THIRTEEN

WEDNESDAY *Bitterness*

*Be kind to one another, tenderhearted,*
*forgiving one another, as God in Christ forgave you.*

Ephesians 4:32

When we walk closely with God we experience one of His most important and powerful graces – self-control. That means when bitterness tries to take up residence in our souls we have His supernatural power to *not* hold onto it but, instead, let it go.

No one in the course of human history has ever been as abused as Jesus was. He was falsely accused, tried and convicted of a crime He didn't commit and then crucified. How did He respond to the horror and unfairness of it all? Did He murmur, complain and get bitter? No! He prayed: *"Forgive them Father for they know not what they do."* Needless to say there'd be a whole lot less hate in the world and fewer wars if we followed His example and were more like Him.

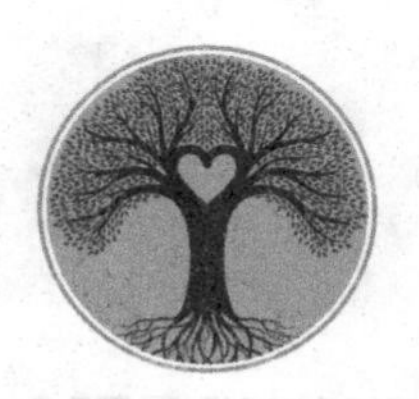

# WEEK THIRTEEN

THURSDAY *Bitterness*

James 3:13-16

Holding onto bitterness is never a good thing. Instead, God wants us to humble ourselves, believe the best about others and let Him fill us with His love, understanding, compassion and mercy. What's important in life is that we obey God and do what He tells us to do. His grace is sufficient and nothing should matter more to us than pleasing Him.

It's not enough to intellectually *know* that holding on to hard feelings is a bad idea. God tells us in His Word to be *doers* of His Word and apply what we know to life. And really, life's too short to do anything less.

# WEEK THIRTEEN

FRIDAY *Bitterness*

*Strive for peace with everyone,*
*and for the holiness without which no one will see the Lord.*

Hebrews 12:14

God tells us how to succeed at life. He teaches us everything, informs and educates, commands and reveals what is wrong and what is right. That's because He loves us and wants us to enjoy living and experience an abundant life. Because that is what He created and saves us for.

What's fascinating is that after we accept Jesus as our personal Savior, He sends His Spirit to take up residence in our souls. It is God's Spirit living in us that makes doing what is *right* and pleasing to God possible. It is by receiving His divine power that we are able to be holy as He is holy.

# WEEK THIRTEEN

SATURDAY/SUNDAY

## Facts of Life:

-Bitterness contaminates our lives.

-Holding on to bitterness and resentment is hazardous to our health.

-Disobedience is sin and sin gets in the way of our intimacy with God.

Personal Reflections:

# WEEK FOURTEEN

MONDAY *Faith*

*Now faith is the assurance of things hoped for,*
*the conviction of things not seen.*
*For by it the people of old received their commendation.*
*By faith we understand that the universe*
*was created by the word of God,*
*so that what is seen was not made out of things that are visible.*

Hebrews 11:1-3

Living by faith is a choice, really. We either choose to believe or we don't. One of the hardest challenges we face as we follow Jesus is that we must set aside human logic and put our absolute trust in Him. Why we foolishly put more faith in ourselves and other people and social systems than we do God...is a mystery. Looking at our track record as human beings can't we see it doesn't work? What would happen if instead of doing things our own way we got to know Jesus really well and obeyed Him? We may just be surprised at how beautiful life would turn out.

# WEEK FOURTEEN

TUESDAY *Faith*

Genesis 6

God told Noah to build an arc, so he did. That could be the end of the story, but there's more.

God created man and, about the time He told Noah to build a boat, He regretted it. The Lord decided to destroy everything He'd created with a flood because man had become so evil and start all over. God enlisted Noah's help because he was one of the few good guys left on earth. God's plan must have sounded bazaar to Noah, but he responded in faith and said "Yes!" to God.

As a result, Jehovah saved a small remnant of humanity. God does the most miraculous things when we say "Yes" to Him.

# WEEK FOURTEEN

WEDNESDAY *Faith*

Joshua 6:1-20

This story sounds a bit crazy, but it's true. Sometimes it's hard for the human mind to comprehend all that God can do. We're in the habit of putting our faith in what we can see, hear and touch with our hands. And being human, we put far too much credence in what we can and do understand.

So is there a better way to live? Sure! God wants us to depend on and put our trust in Him. It's a matter of setting aside self-sufficiency and believing in the love, sovereign power and eternal wisdom of God. The story of what happened at Jericho is a perfect example of the miracles God can perform when we obey and put our faith in Him.

# WEEK FOURTEEN

THURSDAY *Faith*

*For I delivered to you as of first importance what I also received: that Christ died for our sins in accordance with the Scriptures, that he was buried, that he was raised on the third day in accordance with the Scriptures.*

I Corinthians 15:3-4

---

This is the "gospel" message plain and simple. When we believe with our hearts and put our faith in Jesus our sins are forgiven and we know for certain that when we die we will spend eternity in heaven with Him.

The decision we make about Jesus, whether or not we believe in Him, is the most important decision we will ever make. Not only will it determine where we spend eternity but it will also have a huge impact on how we live our lives down here on earth.

# WEEK FOURTEEN

FRIDAY

*Faith*

*For truly, I say to you, if you have faith*
*like a grain of mustard seed,*
*you will say to this mountain,*
*'Move from here to there,' and it will move,*
*and nothing will be impossible for you.*

Matthew 17:20

---

Faith is a powerful and life transforming commodity. Many people get so caught up in the "moving mountains" aspect of Matthew 17:20 that they miss the import of what Jesus is actually saying. The point Jesus is trying to make is that faith is real, supernatural and it works. Believing in what Jesus can do calls down the power of heaven to earth. And that's what changes our lives.

Believing that what God says about Himself in scripture is absolutely true matters. Walking in obedience and faith allows Jesus to show up in all His glory and prove to an unbelieving world that nothing is impossible with Him.

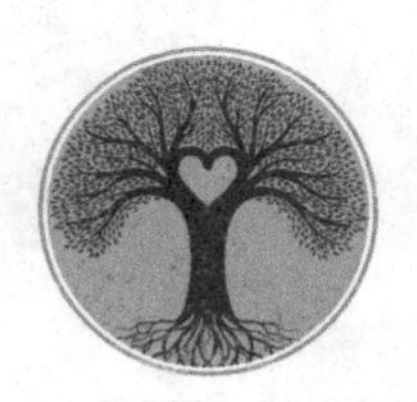

## WEEK FOURTEEN

SATURDAY/SUNDAY

### Facts of Life:

-We were created through life with Jesus and put our faith in Him.

-Believing in Jesus is the most important decision we will ever make.

-Divinely magical things happen when we trust Jesus.

Personal Reflections:

# WEEK FIFTEEN

MONDAY

*Joy*

*Your words were found, and I ate them,*
*and your words became to me a joy*
*and the delight of my heart,*
*for I am called by your name,*
*O Lord, God of hosts.*

Jeremiah 15:16

---

God wanted you, so He made you. He knows you better than you know yourself. He knows who He created you to be and what He equipped you to do; and being the good good Father that He is He continually and tirelessly tries to lead you into the best possible life.

So…with all that said…it shouldn't surprise us that studying His Word would be good for us. Because when we read His words His Spirit can correct our wrong thinking, nourish our spirits, strengthen our hearts and make us whole. So why wouldn't we put ourselves into a position to hear His voice?

# WEEK FIFTEEN

TUESDAY

*Joy*

*The fast of the fourth month and the fast of the fifth and the fast of the seventh and the fast of the tenth shall be to the house of Judah seasons of joy and gladness and cheerful feasts. Therefore love truth and peace.*

Zechariah 8:19

---

"*Love truth and peace*" is the operative phrase in this verse. Unfortunately, we tend to accept worldly philosophies without thinking and embrace man's opinions as fact instead of loving God's truth. Um…but that's not good for us or what God intended when He created us. The lack of peace and joy in our lives proves we're doing something wrong.

Our souls *must* be nourished with God's truth in order for us to thrive. That is how He designed things to be. Abiding in His presence, enjoying His nearness, listening to His voice and obeying *Him* is what we truly need.

## WEEK FIFTEEN

WEDNESDAY

Matthew 25:14-21

---

Loving others as Jesus loves…when we are kind and faithful to use all that God has given us to improve other people's lives… that's when we make a positive difference in the world. *That's joy.*

We belong to God. We were created to serve others and Him and share His eternally good news here on earth. We are a *chosen* people and part of His royal family. We have talents, abilities and strengths that Jesus gave us to use so we can accomplish His purpose and improve conditions in our little corner of the world. But that won't happen until we surrender and have no will of our own.

## WEEK FIFTEEN

THURSDAY

*Joy*

*And he led them out as far as Bethany,*
*and lifting up his hands he blessed them.*
*While he blessed them, he parted from them*
*and was carried up into heaven.*
*And they worshiped him and returned to Jerusalem with great joy.*

Luke 24:50-52

---

Extraordinary things happen when we devote our lives to Jesus. Committing ourselves mind, body and spirit to Him is *the* most powerful means of worship…a way we demonstrate how much we love Him.

Worship isn't just about giving mental ascent to Jesus' existence on Sunday mornings. True heartfelt, world-shaking worship is about knowing God and putting our love for Him into action. The result of living a lifestyle of surrender and devotion to Jesus is *Joy!*

## WEEK FIFTEEN

FRIDAY *Joy*

*Therefore, since we have been justified by faith,*
*we have peace with God through our Lord Jesus Christ.*
*Through him we have also obtained access*
*by faith into this grace in which we stand,*
*and we rejoice in hope of the glory of God.*

Romans 5:1-2

---

When we *believe* in the death, burial and resurrection of Jesus Christ, our sins are forgiven and we are ushered back into God's presence where we will remain forever. The *only* way anyone can be reconciled to God is by placing their faith in Jesus Christ. The decision we make about Jesus is *the* most important decision we will ever make. It is Jesus' unconditional love and redeeming power that makes us truly alive and empowers us to live an abundant life. That is something to celebrate, and loving and being loved by Jesus is our one pure and perfect joy.

## WEEK FIFTEEN

SATURDAY/SUNDAY

| Facts of Life: |
| --- |
| -God knows what we need to thrive. |
| -Loving God's truth leads to great joy. |
| -Rejoice in the Lord! |

Personal Reflections:

# WEEK SIXTEEN

MONDAY

*Lifetime Learner*

*Give your servant therefore an understanding mind*
*to govern your people,*
*that I may discern between good and evil,*
*for who is able to govern this your great people?*

I Kings 3:7-9

---

Solomon was one of the greatest and most influential monarchs in the history of Israel. But as impressive as Solomon was he was still human, imperfect and he needed God's help just like you and me. What stands out in Solomon's personal story is that when he took the throne and the Lord asked him what he wanted most; instead of asking for popularity, fortune and fame, Solomon asked for wisdom. Wisdom is the ability to discern the difference between right and wrong. God gave him what he asked for.

That's one of the greatest challenges we face as humans… admitting to ourselves and, most importantly to God, that we don't know-it-all and can't do-it-all but desperately need His help.

## WEEK SIXTEEN

TUESDAY *Lifetime Learner*

*The LORD by wisdom founded the earth;*
*by understanding he established the heavens;*
*by his knowledge the deeps broke open,*
*and the clouds drop down the dew.*

*My son, do not lose sight of these—*
*keep sound wisdom and discretion,*
*and they will be life for your soul*
*and adornment for your neck.*

Proverbs 3:19-22

God knows *who* and *what* we are because He created us. He watches over us and knows what we go through. He is present and with us. He's God. Understanding that one fundamental fact… we would be fools to sit at His feet and listen to Him?

Humans spend mass amounts of time fixating on their own thoughts…listening to other people's opinions…surfing the web for information they don't really need. But the Lord *our* God is omniscient. He does knows everything. Why is it that we don't turn to Him and learn the truth from the One who made everything, has been around forever and knows it all?

# WEEK SIXTEEN

WEDNESDAY *Lifetime Learner*

*Teach me good judgment and knowledge,*
*for I believe in your commandments.*

Psalm 119:66

---

One of the most incredible things about God is that He promised to teach us everything we need to know if we let Him. In fact, He wants and is waiting to do that very thing. There are many truths He wants to impart to us…lessons we desperately need to learn and a plethora of wisdom and grace He is just waiting to pour into our souls. And He is willing to do for us so we can achieve our full potential as His chosen people, learn and grow into the beautiful and successful people He intended and created us to be. The simplest and most effective way to succeed at life is to listen to God and obey Him.

# WEEK SIXTEEN

THURSDAY *Lifetime Learner*

*But the Helper, the Holy Spirit,*
*whom the Father will send in my name,*
*he will teach you all things*
*and bring to your remembrance all that I have said to you.*

John 14:26

This is a promise from Jesus; a promise that is definitely worth listening to and claiming as our own. After we receive Him as our Savior He sends His Spirit to take up permanent residence in our souls and teaches us everything we need to know. All we have to do is spend time in His presence and study His Word in order for the promise to be fulfilled. That's one of the most beautiful things about our relationship with Jesus is that He provides for our "higher education" and has everything under control.

The true miracle about our unmerited relationship with Jesus is that He cares so much about our future that He is willing to share His love and divine truth with us. Have you ever wondered why He would do such a generous thing?

# WEEK SIXTEEN

FRIDAY *Lifetime Learner*

*Take my instruction instead of silver,*
*and knowledge rather than choice gold,*
*for wisdom is better than jewels,*
*and all that you may desire cannot compare with her.*

Proverbs 8:10-11

---

We have to decide *who* we're going to listen to and *what* we will believe. God gave us a free will and we have a whole lot of important decisions to make when it comes to the living of life. That's the way God planned things from the start. What astounds me is the way God is willing to share His wisdom and knowledge with us. He doesn't have to, but He does. All He requires is that we seek Him with all our hearts and love Him and, of course, study His Word. What I have found utterly amazing is the way it only takes one verse of divine truth a day to fill the emptiness in my soul.

## WEEK SIXTEEN

SATURDAY/SUNDAY *Lifetime Learner*

| Facts of Life: |
|---|
| -God tells us the truth…about everything. |
| -God will teach us what we need to know. |
| -God's thoughts and ways are better than our own. |

Personal Reflections:

# WEEK SEVENTEEN

MONDAY

## *Created by God*

*So God created man in his own image,*
*in the image of God he created him;*
*male and female he created them.*

Genesis 1:27

God made everything, including you and me. How amazing is that? He didn't have to create us, but He did. God the Father, God the Son and the Holy Spirit unanimously decided that it would be a good idea to give us the most precious gift of life. So God made us.

He wants the best for all His children. We are precious in His sight and the piece-de-resistance of His creative genius and divine endeavors. Yes. He loves us. Absolutely! The sad thing is He has to endure a great many heartaches watching us live life on our own, learn and grow. It isn't always a pleasant for Him.

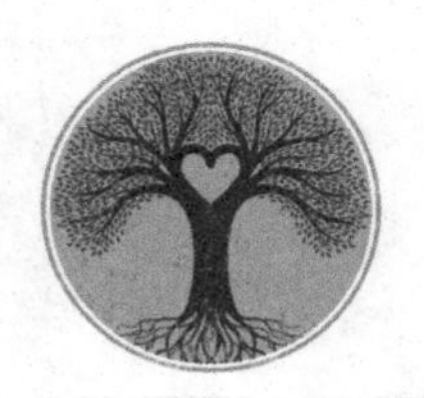

## WEEK SEVENTEEN

TUESDAY *Created by God*

Psalm 139:14-17

---

We did not evolve from some puddle of goo the way some would have us believe. We were wanted by the Sovereign Maker and King of the Universe and personally made *by* Him and *for* Him. He made us for a specific and important reason and we are valuable to Him.

Have you ever wondered what God was thinking when He formed us in our mother's womb? Was He filled with excitement and expectant? Did He look forward to spending a lifetime walking through life at our side? And while He waited for our birth day did He celebrate the one-of-a-kind made in the image of God works of art we would be?

# WEEK SEVENTEEN

WEDNESDAY *Created by God*

*Before I formed you in the womb I knew you,*
*and before you were born I consecrated you;*
*I appointed you a prophet to the nations.*

Jeremiah 1:5

---

God knew us before we were born. *"Knew"* in the sense that, since He personally formed us in our mother's womb, He recognized who and what we would someday be. On top of all that He equipped each one of us with talents, abilities and gifts so we could succeed at life. Of course the key to our success is living according to His plan, not our own.

True peace and the fullness of joy belongs to those who are true to God and their God-given identity. Celebrate! God is good.

# WEEK SEVENTEEN

THURSDAY *Created by God*

*The* L*ORD* *appeared to him from far away.*
*I have loved you with an everlasting love;*
*therefore I have continued my faithfulness to you.*

Jeremiah 31:3

---

God's love is infinite and eternal. He doesn't love us one day and turn His back on us the next. He doesn't fall *in* and, then, *out* of love with us the way humans tend to do. His love is unconditional, fiercely devout and is not based on our performance. We'd be doomed if it were. No. God's love is divine, supernatural and perfect. He loved us even before we were conceived or existed. He wanted us knowing that we would ignore Him, rebel against His will at times and disobey.

God's love is different than anything we've ever experienced and known. That should renew our hope and encourage our souls.

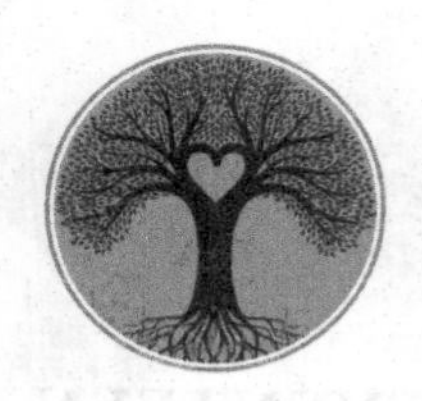

# WEEK SEVENTEEN

FRIDAY *Created by God*

*You shall love the* LORD *your God*
*with all your heart and with all your soul*
*and with all your might.*

Deuteronomy 6:5

---

We were created *by* God, *for* God. That's a fact we forget and too frequently ignore. Life isn't about us contrary to the world's erroneous philosophy. It's about loving and serving our Creator and Lord.

If we want to live the abundant life Jesus died to give us we have to get back to living life the way He intended it to be lived. We were created to love God with our whole heart…with every thought we think, every word we speak and every act we perform.

Sure we're human and get off tract sometimes, but when we return to God He promised to open the windows of heaven and pour out onto us more blessings than we can receive (Malachi 3:6-10).

## WEEK SEVENTEEN

SATURDAY/SUNDAY *Created by God*

### Facts of Life:

-God wanted us so He created us.

-We are handmade by God works of art.

-God's love is forever.

Personal Reflections:

# WEEK EIGHTTEEN

MONDAY *Disappointments*

Psalm 46:1-5

Trouble happens. It's one of those unfortunate facts of life. Accepting this reality humbles our self-centered spirits and frees us up to ask for God's help. He's always "there" for us. He always has been and He always will be.

King Solomon, in the Book of Ecclesiastes, wrote that *two are better than one.* Jesus is our partner in life. We can run *to* Him or turn away from Him. We can ask for His wisdom and help or try to figure everything out on our own. But Jesus knows what we're going through, sympathizes with our many weaknesses and is willing to help. He's on our side. Why wouldn't He?

# WEEK EIGHTTEEN

TUESDAY *Disappointments*

*Be still, and know that I am God.*
*I will be exalted among the nations,*
*I will be exalted in the earth!*

Psalm 46:10

When we're in trouble it's important for us to turn to Jesus and fix our undivided attention on Him. But we have a problem. We've gotten into the bad habit of trying to deal with life on our own. But self-sufficiency rarely, if ever, works. We weren't designed to go it alone. God created us to do life *with* Him. When we get into trouble we need to sit down with Jesus' and be still. When we do the Holy Spirit has a chance to open our eyes to the truth, give us a new and better perspective on our circumstances and lead us in the direction He wants us to go. It's astounding the benefits being still and opening ourselves up to Jesus may produce.

# WEEK EIGHTTEEN

WEDNESDAY *Disappointments*

*Now is my soul troubled. And what shall I say?*
*'Father, save me from this hour'?*
*But for this purpose I have come to this hour.*

John 12:27

Jesus was troubled and sometimes felt overwhelmed. Yes, He knew what He was getting Himself into when He left heaven and came to He understood that He would be persecuted by the people He created, loved and would die for on a cross for their sin. But His knowing these things beforehand didn't negate that He would physically, emotionally and mentally hurt. Humanly I don't think we can even begin to imagine the suffering He endured on our behalf. Perhaps, in His darkest hours Jesus demonstrated how we are to deal with the great and often overwhelming challenges of life. We can learn a lot from Him.

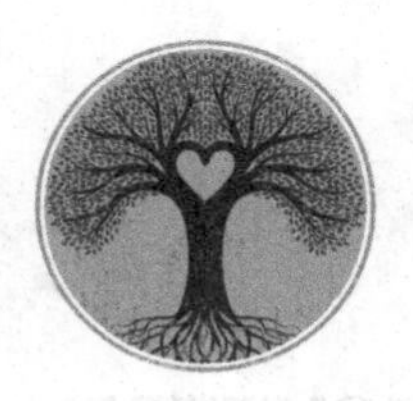

# WEEK EIGHTTEEN

THURSDAY *Disappointments*

*My grace is sufficient for you,*
*for my power is made perfect in weakness.*
*Therefore I will boast all the more gladly of my weaknesses,*
*so that the power of Christ may rest upon me.*

II Corinthians 12:9

---

Everyone experiences disappointments. We will all get hurt, be disappointed and have problems. The good news is that the apostle Paul tells us how to prepare ourselves for the inevitable. It's all about inviting Jesus into the center of our lives and letting Him guide our steps and have His way every step of the way.

When bad stuff happens it has a tendency to get us off balance and make us afraid. But instead of obsessing on our circumstances, what if we asked God for help? What if we put all our trust in Him and allow Him to wipe away our confusion and get us back on tract? Pretty simple, right?

# WEEK EIGHTTEEN

FRIDAY

*Disappointments*

*I can do all things through him who strengthens me.*

Philippians 4:13

---

We can succeed, because Jesus is with us and on our side. That means, because of Him, we can do anything He asks us to do and whatever needs to be done. We can heal from past hurts, right wrongs that have been done to us and forgive the unforgiveable. We can learn and grow and become far more than we ever imagined. But first we have to stop being self-sufficient and relying on ourselves. Instead we have the glorious privilege of leaning into Jesus and walking by faith and depending on His grace and His grace alone. With Jesus on our side we can even change the world. What a relief to know there's hope.

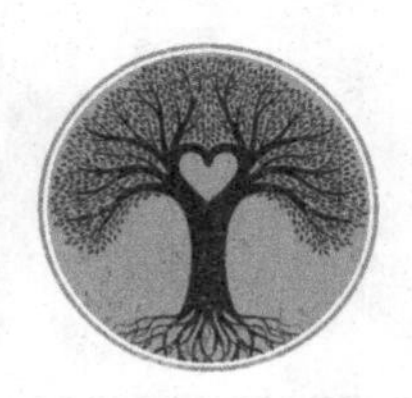

## WEEK EIGHTTEEN

SATURDAY/SUNDAY *Disappointments*

Facts of Life:

-Trouble happens.

-God is there for us.

-God knows what we need.

Personal Reflections:

# WEEK NINETEEN

MONDAY *Submission*

*"And going a little farther he fell on his face and prayed, saying, 'My Father, if it be possible, let this cup pass from me; nevertheless, not as I will, but as you will.'"*

Matthew 26:39

---

Jesus submitted to His Father's will. He wasn't necessarily looking forward to being crucified for our sin, but did what needed to be done. Jesus' prayer in the Garden of Gethsemene gives us a glimpse at the agony He endured on our behalf.

The real gift of this story, however, is the way Jesus denied Himself and did what His Father wanted Him to do. The lesson for us is simple. We can *feel* what we feel. That is not a sin. But in the end we are to put ourselves under God's authority and submit ourselves wholeheartedly to His will.

## WEEK NINETEEN

TUESDAY *Submission*

*May grace and peace be multiplied to you.*

I Peter 1:1-2

---

We were chosen by God to obey. Obedience. It sounds simple. We know it is not. It's our rebellion that gets us into trouble. That's because of sin. But God's ways are not our ways. They're better. When He says "love one another," that's what we're supposed to do. It's up to us whether or not we obey.

Yes, sometimes God tells us to do something that seems impossible and outside the box. What we must know and understand is that He provides is with everything we need to obey. Always and forever He will give us the courage and strength to make the right choice and do the right thing. To God be the glory.

# WEEK NINETEEN

WEDNESDAY *Submission*

*Likewise, husbands, live with your wives in an understanding way,*
*showing honor to the woman as the weaker vessel,*
*since they are heirs with you of the grace of life,*
*so that your prayers may not be hindered.*

I Peter 3:7

---

Everyone has to submit to somebody. Putting ourselves under someone's authority is just a part of life. When God made everything He put the whole principle into motion. And because of our inherited sin nature we've been resisting it ever since.

What we have to understand is that submission isn't about taking away our freedom or preventing us from living an abundant life. Actually the opposite is true. Submitting to God and doing things His way is the one and only way we can ever be truly free, achieve our divine potential and accomplish the good works He intended us to do.

God knows what He's doing. We only think we do.

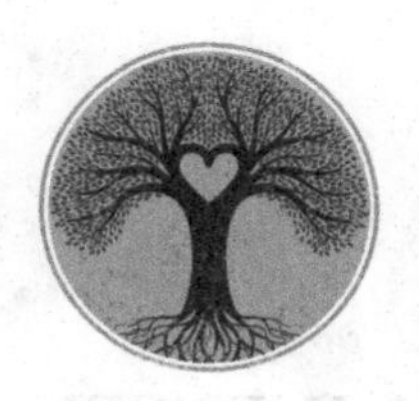

# WEEK NINETEEN

THURSDAY *Submission*

*I appeal to you therefore, brothers, by the mercies of God,*
*to present your bodies as a living sacrifice,*
*holy and acceptable to God, which is your spiritual worship.*

Romans 12:1

---

We love God, and we prove that we love God by submitting to Him. Putting ourselves under His authority is the ultimate form of worship, really. Letting God be God and submitting to Him is a privilege and the role we were designed to play. Resisting the will of God and fighting against Him only creates chaos, frustration and only makes life terribly hard. Everything would be a whole lot easier if we just lived the way God intended us to live. Besides, when we say "YES!" to God there is peace and a whole lot of joy.

# WEEK NINETEEN

FRIDAY

*Submission*

I Peter 2:13-15

Submission - Whether we put ourselves under the authority of a spouse, pastor or employer, ultimately, we are putting ourselves under the authority of and submitting to God. He is sovereign and the One who gives any and all authority to men.

So what if we submitted to God and, instead of aggressively competing in the work place trying to climb the corporate ladder, what if we honored each other and worked as a team. In personal relationships, instead of adopting an adversarial attitude, what would happen if we cooperated and thought more about others than we do ourselves? Life in general, on every level, could get a whole lot easier and sweeter if we submitted to God and placed ourselves under His grace and control.

## WEEK NINETEEN

SATURDAY/SUNDAY

| Facts of Life: |
| --- |
| -Jesus did what His Father told Him to do. |
| -We have to surrender every minute of every day, today and for the rest of our lives. |
| -Submission honors God and pleases Him. |

Personal Reflections:

# WEEK TWENTY

MONDAY

*Humility*

*He has told you, O man, what is good;*
*and what does the LORD require of you*
*but to do justice, and to love kindness,*
*and to walk humbly with your God?*

Micah 6:8

---

God loves us! Now that *is* good news. "News" we should appreciate and celebrate. Our Heavenly Father wants the best for His children. He is committed to leading us into the abundant life He planned for us to enjoy. And He longs to shower us with His love, favor and mercy today, tomorrow and every day of our lives. But although God is a *giver* by virtue of His divine nature and loves us unconditionally, there is something He requires of you and me - Humility.

That's not exactly a word we're comfortable with in this self-absorbed day and age. Still, humility is important to God and, therefore, it must be important to us.

# WEEK TWENTY

TUESDAY *Humility*

*Take my yoke upon you, and learn from me,*
*for I am gentle and lowly in heart,*
*and you will find rest for your souls.*
*For my yoke is easy, and my burden is light.*

Matthew 11:29-30

---

Some people think that being humble is an archaic notion. They're wrong of course! Jesus was humble and gave His life away to save our souls. Humility is a God-honoring timeless spiritual virtue.

When Jesus walked the earth He faced many hardships and experienced everything we do and more. He rubbed shoulders with the arrogant, the prideful and witnessed untold atrocities and violence. He still humbled Himself to the point of death and died for our sin. He didn't flaunt or abuse His rights and privileges as the Son of God. He lived a quiet, gentle and uncompromising life that attracted people and ushered them into His kingdom instead. What could be more important and precious than that?

# WEEK TWENTY

WEDNESDAY *Humility*

*Incline your ear, O LORD, and answer me,*
*for I am poor and needy.*

Psalm 86:1

When we accept that we are finite beings: weak, poor and needy, it is a step in the right direction. The world tells us we can be anything we want to be and do anything we set our minds to. But that's not true. We are created beings, fallen creatures who are infected with all sorts of limitations and flaws. We can fantasize about *having-it-all* and delude ourselves into thinking we can live successfully without God's help, but we can't. We need God. That is a fact of life and the way He intended things to be.

Humbling ourselves before God and asking for His help is key to living life abundantly...a sign of strength, not weakness.

## WEEK TWENTY

THURSDAY

*Humility*

*Likewise, you who are younger, be subject to the elders.*
*Clothe yourselves, all of you, with humility toward one another,*
*for God opposes the proud but gives grace to the humble.*

I Peter 5:5

---

Pride is a sin and God cannot look upon sin. And when you stop and think about it why are we so puffed up and full of ourselves?

Scripture says that God fights against those who think more highly of themselves than they ought to. There's a fine line between walking "confidently" through life in a God-honoring way and taking all the credit for who we are and what we do. The arrogant person says, "Look how great I am." The humble person's life points people to Jesus and celebrates His love and grace. He alone is worthy of grace.

# WEEK TWENTY

FRIDAY *Humility*

*Do nothing from selfish ambition or conceit,*
*but in humility count others more significant than yourselves.*

Philippians 2:3

We are all unique, special and valuable in God's eyes. All of that is by God's creative genius and divine design. And He made us the way we are deliberately, for a reason. The beauty and diversity of humanity is truly something we should appreciate and celebrate.

What is exceptional in the eternal scheme of things is that it doesn't matter whether you are the Queen of England or a homeless drug addict on the street; God has a plan for each life. He longs to bless everyone and fill us with the fullness of Himself and shower our spirits with hope. We are valuable and precious because we belong to Him.

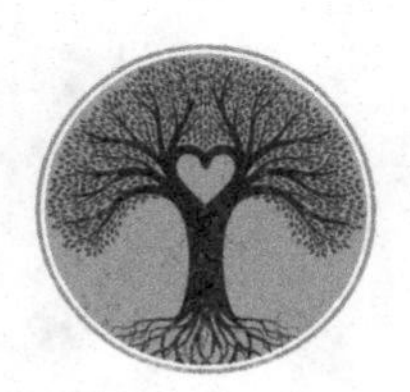

## WEEK TWENTY

SATURDAY/SUNDAY

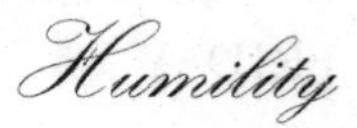


### Facts of Life:

-God loves us!

-Accepting that we are poor and needy
is a step in the right direction.

-God fights against pride but gives grace to the humble.

Personal Reflections:

# WEEK TWENTY ONE

MONDAY *Solitude and Silence*

*Be still, and know that I am God.*
*I will be exalted among the nations,*
*I will be exalted in the earth!*

Psalm 46:10

---

Solitude isn't just about running *away* from people and being alone. It's about disengaging from our earthly circumstances and responsibilities for a time so we can spend quality time with Jesus. "My life is too busy." That's what some people say. It seems to be the gut-wrenching cry of the twenty first century. But we deceive ourselves. We abuse ourselves by engaging in non-stop activity and taking on too much. The erroneous notion that life is about going and doing and producing and accomplishing is wrong! It's not. That's not what God intended when He created us. So He whispers, "*Be still and know that I am God.*" The question we have to ask ourselves is, "Will we?"

# WEEK TWENTY ONE

TUESDAY *Solitude and Silence*

*In these days he went out to the mountain to pray,*
*and all night he continued in prayer to God.*

Luke 6:12

When we disengage from the world and meet with God face to face…that's when we are able to immerse ourselves completely in His presence and fully enjoy His love. In the midst of all the chaos that *is* our earthly existence, these special and sacred moments of solitude provide what our souls desperately need and crave. Solitude isn't a luxury. It's an absolute necessity if we want to live a God-honoring life.

Besides the benefits we personally derive from spending time with Jesus, have you ever stopped to think about how much He enjoys those precious and sacred moment and how they make Him smile?

# WEEK TWENTY ONE

WEDNESDAY *Solitude and Silence*

*Now when Jesus heard this,*
*he withdrew from there in a boat to a desolate place by himself.*
*But when the crowds heard it, they followed*
*him on foot from the towns.*
*When he went ashore he saw a great crowd,*
*and he had compassion on them and healed their sick.*

Matthew 14:13-14

---

In scripture we see Jesus withdrawing from society to a solitary place so He could spend time with His Father. Spending time with God is always appropriate and a good idea. Life is full and there are always issues to work through, disappointments to recover from, joys and sorrows to deal with and decisions to make. The good news is that God is interested and we can share all of them with Him. In fact we're supposed to. God wants us to. Solitude provides us with a perfect opportunity to set our minds on heavenly matters, receive His power and experience His love. Those incredible moments we spend with Him refocuses our attention on what matters most.

# WEEK TWENTY ONE

THURSDAY *Solitude and Silence*

*And they went away in the boat to a desolate place by themselves.*

Mark 6:32

Mark's message is simple and to the point. The fast paced life we live in this contemporary age is ludicrous and insane. We are self-destructing and abusing ourselves by not giving ourselves permission to just be and slow down.

Jesus was far more important, busier and productive than we will ever be. He was also a master at establishing healthy boundaries to protect the sacredness of His life. He accomplished an extraordinary body of good works in the relatively short three and a half years He spent in ministry. He loved, taught, healed, encouraged, raised people from the grave and started His church. More significantly He accomplished exactly what His Father sent Him to earth to do. We would do well if we followed His example.

# WEEK TWENTY ONE

FRIDAY *Solitude and Silence*

*And when you pray, you must not be like the hypocrites.*
*For they love to stand and pray in the*
*synagogues and at the street corners,*
*that they may be seen by others. Truly, I say to you,*
*they have received their reward. But when you pray,*
*go into your room and shut the door and*
*pray to your Father who is in secret.*
*And your Father who sees in secret will reward you.*

Matthew 6:5-6

---

Everyone wants to be blessed by God. It's only natural. What's divinely magical is that He wants to do that very thing. When He tells us to go to a quiet place and pray, He's telling us to do something that's good for us.

Spending time with Jesus isn't just about entering His presence with a long list of what we want and think He needs to do. Prayer is about relating to God and developing intimacy with Him… enjoying Him…learning how to listen and receiving *from* Him what He chooses to give. It is during the sacred moments we spend with God that we are favored and truly blessed.

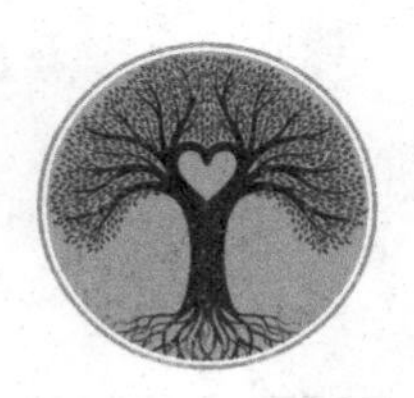

# WEEK TWENTY ONE

SATURDAY/SUNDAY *Solitude and Silence*

Facts of Life:

-Silence and solitude is about drawing near to God so He can draw near to you.

-Going to a quiet place and spending time with God in prayer is the best thing you can do.

-There is nothing Jesus cannot do.

Personal Reflections:

# WEEK TWENTY TWO

MONDAY *Sin*

*There is no one righteous, not even one;*
*there is no one who understands;*
*there is no one who seeks God.*

Romans 3:10-11 (NIV)

We're all sinners. We may not enjoy the idea or understand the theological facts behind it, but it's still true. Adam and Eve rebelled against God and rejected the perfect plan He had for their lives. Consequently, we inherited their sin nature and predisposition to rebel.

It is that sin-nature we inherited from Adam that separates us from God. That's why Jesus died on a cross and paid the penalty for our sin. He wanted to save us from spiritual death so we could spend eternity in heaven with Him and live an abundant life. The Lord Jesus did for us what we could not do for ourselves.

Thank You, Jesus.

# WEEK TWENTY TWO

TUESDAY *Sin*

*But God shows his love for us*
*in that while we were still sinners,*
*Christ died for us.*

Romans 5:8

---

It's beyond imagining the way Jesus died for our sin. He didn't wait for us to get our act together. He knew we couldn't and wouldn't. We could never be good enough to earn our way back into His good graces. We are after all only feeble and finite human beings. So Jesus came to earth and did for us what we could not do for ourselves.

He did the incomprehensible because He cares. The Bible says He wanted to bless us with the chance to have a personal relationship with Him and experience an abundant life. That's why He did what He did. Truly the whole thing is way too incredible for the human mind to comprehend.

# WEEK TWENTY TWO

WEDNESDAY *Sin*

*For my eyes are on all their ways.*
*They are not hidden from me,*
*nor is their iniquity concealed from my eyes.*

Jeremiah 16:17

God knows everything there is to know about us and loves us anyway. Isn't that amazing? His love is unconditional but, at the same time, refuses to leave us where we are. He has high expectations and great plans for us. He created us, saves our souls, corrects, teaches, reshapes and tirelessly works to conform us to the image of His pure and perfect Son. On top of all that He promises that He will finish the good work He started in us.

God wants the best for you and is willing to fill you with divine power and make you whole. All you have to do is let Him.

## WEEK TWENTY TWO

THURSDAY *Sin*

*For His eyes are upon the ways of man,*
*and He sees all his steps.*

Job 34:21 (NAS)

The world is infected with evil, depravity and sin. We're not supposed to be a part of it. We belong to Jesus. We're different and supposed to live our lives in a way that pleases and honors Him. It may seem like a tall order but it *is* absolutely doable when we put our trust in Him and rely totally on His supernatural help. He promises that His grace is sufficient. His strength is made perfect in our weakness and we can do all things through Him.

studying God's Word is essential if we want to achieve our divine potential and live in a way that brings attention to Him.

# WEEK TWENTY TWO

FRIDAY *Sin*

*If we confess our sins,*
*he is faithful and just to forgive us our sins*
*and to cleanse us from all unrighteousness.*

I John 1:9

---

God is the only one who can forgive our sin and cleanse us from the inside out. And He will do that very thing if we humble ourselves, confess our sin and ask Him to. We are His children. He loves us and is faithful.

Sin isn't a pleasant subject, but it is one we cannot afford to ignore. It's our responsibility to maintain our spiritual health and take good care of our souls. We take care of our bodies. Why wouldn't we take care of our souls? So we go to the Lord and talk to Him about, agree with Him when we have sinned. We don't want anything to get in the way of our sweet relationship with Him.

# WEEK TWENTY TWO

SATURDAY/SUNDAY

Facts of Life:

-We've all sinned.

-We live in the world but we're not supposed to be a part of it.

-God will forgive our sin if we confess our sin and ask.

Personal Reflections:

# WEEK TWENTY THREE

MONDAY

*Prayer*

*Behold, I stand at the door and knock.*
*If anyone hears my voice and opens the door,*
*I will come in to him and eat with him, and he with me.*

Revelation 3:20

---

Prayer is a way to connect and communicate with God. By entering into the sacred rite of prayer we open our heart to God, enjoy the One who made us and get to know Him. When we wake up and before we go to bed at night we should turn our attention in His direction and reach out for Him.

But is that what we do? Do we share our lives with the One who gave us life? Prayer, really, is an ongoing conversation between the Creator and created; a conversation that never ends. The door to God's throne room is always open and we can enter into His presence 24/7. He is our Father. He is genuinely interested in what we're doing, how we feel and what we think.

# WEEK TWENTY THREE

TUESDAY *Prayer*

*Before they call I will answer;*
*while they are yet speaking I will hear.*

Isaiah 65:24

The Almighty God of the Universe and Maker of Heaven and Earth promised to hear our prayers and answer them. Think about how extraordinary that is. He made us and cares deeply about us. He didn't create us and then launch us into the Universe to do life on our own. That was not God's intention or how His plan works. He wants to have a personal relationship with us and actively participate in our lives. He's always with us and we are not alone. What's more we can talk to God about anything and everything. Now that is amazing, indeed.

# WEEK TWENTY THREE

WEDNESDAY

*Prayer*

*I am the vine; you are the branches.*
*Whoever abides in me and I in him,*
*he it is that bears much fruit,*
*for apart from me you can do nothing.*

John 15:5

---

Contrary to popular opinion we cannot do anything of any true and lasting value apart from Jesus. According to Jesus that is the truth. That's one of the reasons why everyone desperately needs God in their lives, not only to survive, but to thrive. And that is where prayer comes in.

Prayer changes things; more importantly it changes us. In God's company our thinking is reformed, our perspective dramatically altered and God's Spirit enables us to see ourselves and others and life through His eyes. He wants to bless us with Himself.

## WEEK TWENTY THREE

THURSDAY *Prayer*

*What causes quarrels and what causes fights among you?*
*Is it not this, that your passions are at war within you?*
*You desire and do not have, so you murder.*
*You covet and cannot obtain, so you fight and quarrel.*
*You do not have, because you do not ask.*
*You ask and do not receive, because you ask wrongly,*
*to spend it on your passions.*

James 4:1-3

We can talk to God about anything, and everything. He loves us unconditionally and perfectly and longs to provide for our every need. And He is the only one who is aware of what we truly need.

We're human and bound to earth by many things. We are vulnerable, susceptible and easily overtaken by the dangers that exist in this ol' world. That makes it hard for us to stay spiritually fit and keep our minds set on the things of heaven. But God can and will help. All we need to do is to turn to Him.

# WEEK TWENTY THREE

FRIDAY

*Prayer*

*Jesus answered him,*
*"What I am doing you do not understand now,*
*but afterward you will understand."*

John 13:7

We pray. We wait. Time passes. And sometimes it seems like maybe God didn't hear. But God did hear and is working. His answer is on its way. Sometimes He says "Yes." Sometimes He says "No." And there are times when He says "Not right now, I want you to wait a while." God has a plan for our lives and it is perfect. The answers to our prayers can come wrapped in different kinds of packages. But we can rest and trust in the fact that our heavenly Father sees, hears and knows everything. The key is to trust Him with our whole heart.

# WEEK TWENTY THREE

SATURDAY/SUNDAY

Facts of Life:

-Prayer connects us to Jesus.

-God cares and listens.

-We can talk to God about anything.

Personal Reflections:

# WEEK TWENTY FOUR

MONDAY

*God's Voice*

John 10:25-30

God speaks to those who take the time to listen. Why wouldn't He? He created us. He loves us. He's always wanted and intended to be a part of our lives. He has many wonderful and important things He longs to tell us…facts about life, heaven and hell, words that will guide our every step and heal our hearts. The desire of His heart is to make us whole.

When Jesus died on the cross for our sin it was only the beginning of His involvement in our lives. He came to earth to save our souls from hell. Yes! That is true. But the Bible also says that He sent His Spirit to live in us when we surrender our lives to Him. Why would He go to all that trouble and, then, be silent? He wouldn't. That's the point.

# WEEK TWENTY FOUR

TUESDAY *God's Voice*

*Or do you not know that your body*
*is a temple of the Holy Spirit within you,*
*whom you have from God? You are not your own,*
*for you were bought with a price.*
*So glorify God in your body.*

I Corinthians 6:19-20

What a miracle! There's no way to wrap our minds around such an extraordinary thing. Why would God send His Spirit to live in us? Why would the Maker of Heaven and Earth want to be that close and involved in each of our lives? But He did. And He does. The minute we put our faith in Jesus it's all about doing life together with Him; the good, the bad and, yes, even the ugly. He truly cares more about each one of us than we can ever imagine.

Have you spent time with Jesus lately? Life is so much sweeter and easier when we do.

# WEEK TWENTY FOUR

WEDNESDAY *God's Voice*

*Incline your ear, and come to me;*
*hear, that your soul may live;*
*and I will make with you an everlasting covenant,*
*my steadfast, sure love for David.*

Isaiah 55:3

---

God invites us to talk to and learn *from* Him. He longs for us to stop all our unnecessary running around long enough so we can hear His voice and enjoy His presence.

The unexpected beauty of Isaiah 55:3 is that God is talking to you and to me. The Almighty God of the Universe is personally inviting us to draw close and spend quality time with Him. Why wouldn't we? We don't deserve to sit down and talk with God. He invites and welcomes us in anyway. We didn't earn the right to enter His throne room and hear His voice. Our connectedness with God is a sacred gift from God and God alone. How could there be a more humbling and thrilling gift?

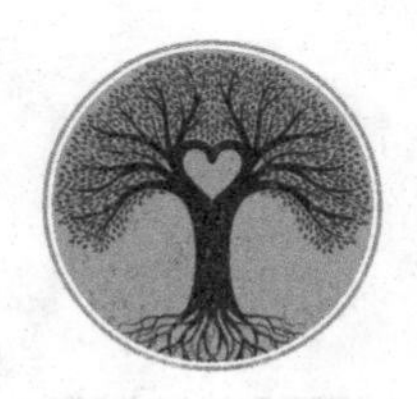

# WEEK TWENTY FOUR

THURSDAY

*God's Voice*

*The glory that you have given me I have given to them,*
*that they may be one even as we are one,*
*I in them and you in me,*
*that they may become perfectly one,*
*so that the world may know that you sent me*
*and loved them even as you loved me.*

John 17:22-23

From God's eternal perspective our relationship with Him is what matters most in life. To Him our very existence is all about cultivating intimacy with Him. He made us *for* Himself. He died to save our souls from hell so we could know, love and enjoy Him and live with Him in heaven forever.

Yes, we have the privilege of entering God's presence and talking to Him. The problem is we forget that prayer is a two way street. Prayer isn't just about talking *to* God. Far more importantly it's about learning how to listen, recognize and obey His voice.

# WEEK TWENTY FOUR

FRIDAY *God's Voice*

*Therefore, behold, I will allure her,*
*and bring her into the wilderness,*
*and speak tenderly to her.*

Hosea 2:14

---

God is the gentle lover of our souls. His Word provides us with nourishment, sustenance, strength and hope. We do Him a great disservice when we think of Him as a harsh and abusive taskmaster, always angry, shouting out commands and bossing us around. In the Book of Hosea we see God's tenderness towards His people on display. He is kind and compassionate. He is holy, the quintessential perfect parent, a faithful companion and tenderhearted lover all rolled into one. Whether He speaks to us in His Word or through His Spirit, via circumstances or the wise counsel of a trusted friend, He eagerly waits to tell us the truth about many things. All we have to do is learn how to listen by slowing down.

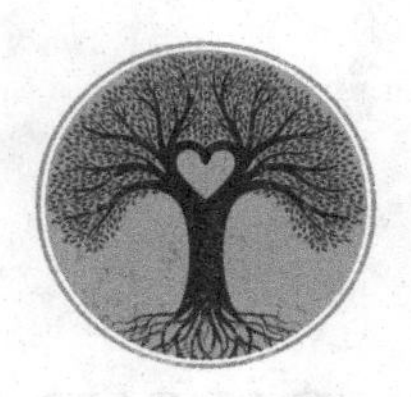

# WEEK TWENTY FOUR

SATURDAY/SUNDAY *God's Voice*

## Facts of Life:

-God speaks

-God invites us to listen to Him

-God is the gentle, faithful and tenderhearted love of our souls

Personal Reflections:

# WEEK TWENTY FIVE

MONDAY

*Children*

*And he took a child and put him in the midst of them,*
*and taking him in his arms, he said to them,*
*"Whoever receives one such child in my name receives me,*
*and whoever receives me, receives not me but him who sent me."*

Mark 9:36-37

---

The words *"taking the child in His arms"* are exceptionally revealing. They let us see into the very heart of God. He meant them to touch us in the deepest and hidden places inside our hearts. Many of us never felt loved or cherished as a child...never felt cared about or cared for. Often parents get so overwhelmed with the demands of everyday living they are emotionally unavailable. In turn, that can cause emotional wounds and brokenness in a young person's life. But there's hope. Every one of us can find healing and wholeness in Jesus. He is the one we most need and are looking for. Everyone, no matter how young or old, is valuable in His sight and important to Him.

# WEEK TWENTY FIVE

TUESDAY *Children*

*Train up a child in the way he should go;*
*even when he is old he will not depart from it.*

Proverbs 22:6

The child who is raised in a Christ centered home and has personally experienced His unconditional love first hand is at a huge advantage. Yes, they still have to believe in the death, burial and resurrection of Jesus and surrender their lives to Him in order to know Him personally and receive His gift of salvation. But because they have heard Jesus' name spoken out loud in their homes and seen their parents honor Him the step of faith required is often easier for them. The beautiful incredible fact of life is that Jesus' love excludes no one. Regardless of what we experienced in our family of origin, His mercy is available to all. He loves and died for everyone.

# WEEK TWENTY FIVE

WEDNESDAY *Children*

*Hear this, you elders;*
*give ear, all inhabitants of the land!*
*Has such a thing happened in your days,*
*or in the days of your fathers?*
*Tell your children of it,*
*and let your children tell their children,*
*and their children to another generation.*

Joel 1:2-3

---

Talking about Jesus and telling others about all the great things He's done in our lives is important. Our personal story and the verbal spiritual heritage we pass down from one generation to the next perpetuates faith. Speaking boldly and confidently about the miracles Jesus has performed in our lives alerts children of all ages to the reality of Jesus and the work He is doing in the world. It's a simple and effective way of handing down a legacy of faith to our families. Honoring Jesus and not being ashamed to speak well of Him is far more valuable than any material possession or impressive bank account we can leave as an inheritance.

Children and grandchildren need to know we love Jesus and that they are loved by Him.

# WEEK TWENTY FIVE

THURSDAY *Children*

John 21:15-17

Do I love Jesus more than anyone and anything? That's the question we have to ask ourselves. Do we love Him enough to tell others about His saving grace and help them develop a personal and intimate relationship with Him? Do we value His mercy enough to give up everything so we can spend our lives studying His Word and serving Him?

That's what Jesus was talking to Peter about in today's passage. Think of a baby lamb – how vulnerable and dependent they are. They need food to eat and water to drink. They need someone to watch over them and protect them from harm. Baby lambs are like little children. Everyone is supposed to "feed" God's sheep. People's eternity is on the line.

# WEEK TWENTY FIVE

FRIDAY

*Children*

*My son, do not forget my teaching,*
*but let your heart keep my commandments.*

Proverbs 3:1

Wisdom produces well-being deep within our souls. We're all God's children. He is our Father. He made us. We belong to Him. We can trust Him. When we read His Word and receive His instruction and obey Him we are blessed. It's all about *making* the time to sit quietly at His feet and learn from Him. That is a privilege, necessary and right.

Before we can be a good parent we have to learn how to be a good child. How can we raise up our children in the way they should go if we don't live the way the Lord would have us live?

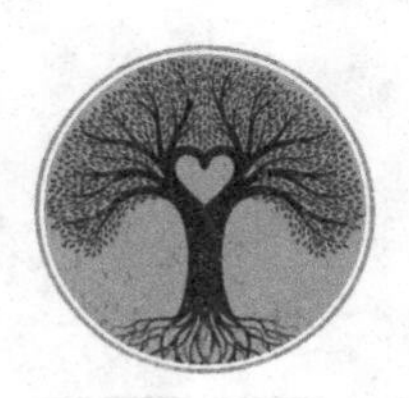

# WEEK TWENTY FIVE

SATURDAY/SUNDAY

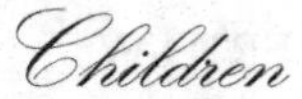


## Facts of Life:

-We are all God's children and valuable to Him.

-Children who are raised to love Jesus are at an advantage.

-Talking about Jesus and the great things He's done
Is the greatest legacy we can leave our children.

Personal Reflections:

# WEEK TWENTY SIX

MONDAY *God's Word*

*All Scripture is breathed out by God*
*and profitable for teaching, for reproof, for correction,*
*and for training in righteousness,*

II Timothy 3:16

---

Every book, chapter and verse in the Bible, from Genesis to Revelation, is inspired by God and, therefore, one hundred percent accurate and true. Every single word of scripture originated in the heart and mind of God. It is perfect just as He is perfect. There are no exceptions to this marvelous fact of life. It is a relief to know that God tells us the truth about everything and that His Spirit teaches us what we need to know about life, love, personal excellence and how to receive and enjoy being loved by Him. We belong to Him and that is what makes life so precious.

We get ourselves in all sorts of trouble by thinking we're smarter than Him.

## WEEK TWENTY SIX

TUESDAY *God's Word*

*Your word is a lamp to my feet*
*and a light to my path.*

Psalm 119:105

God's light of love and brilliance shines brightly into every age and at all times. His light is shining right now in this confused, dark and lonely world. God's Word illuminates the path that is our life and leads us into a brighter tomorrow that is filled with faith, courage and hope.

God is with us morning, noon and night. He is whispering words of love and encouragement over us this very moment. Are we listening? If we ask for His help, He will help us. If we ask for wisdom, His Spirit will guide our steps and bless us with insight and understanding. We don't have to be great theologians and Bible scholars to read God's Word and reap its rewards. The Lord promised that His Spirit would teach us everything we need to know.

# WEEK TWENTY SIX

WEDNESDAY

*God's Word*

*Do your best to present yourself to God*
*as one approved, a worker who has no need to be ashamed,*
*rightly handling the word of truth.*

II Timothy 2:15

---

Life is about seeking, knowing, and enjoying the Lord. In order for that to happen we must study His Word. Reading the Bible and learning the truth is one of the most important things we will ever do. Our relationship with Jesus *is* life and means everything. Besides – If we don't spend time with Jesus how will we ever learn the truth about life? When and how will we learn the truth about Jesus? How will we learn how to love one another and become the people God intended and needs us to be?

Spending time with Jesus in His Word *is* the life's blood of our relationship with Him. We're lost without it. Allelujah, Amen.

## WEEK TWENTY SIX

THURSDAY *God's Word*

*Open my eyes, that I may behold*
*wondrous things out of your law.*

Psalm 119:18

---

What a precious and practical prayer. We ask God to *"open our eyes,"* and He does. We ask Him to tell us the truth, and He will. Why wouldn't He? He wrote the Bible *to* us and *for* us…in order to draw us close, tell us the truth and share Himself with us. When we open our Bibles and study…His Spirit *reforms* our thinking and replaces confusion, anxieties and unhappiness with peace, joy and hope. We can learn so much from God. Why wouldn't we listen to Him?

# WEEK TWENTY SIX

FRIDAY

*God's Word*

*I will praise you with an upright heart,*
*when I learn your righteous rules.*
*I will keep your statutes;*
*do not utterly forsake me!*

Psalm 119:7-8

Everyone wants to live an abundant life, right? Well, that's exactly why Jesus came to earth and died for our sin. It wasn't just so we could escape hell and get into heaven, although that is part of it. He sacrificed His life so we could live a new and better life *in, for* and *with* Him.

When we accept Jesus as our personal Savior it isn't the end of something. It's just the beginning of a personal, intimate and eternal relationship with Him…a new, different and far better way of life. He wants to help us achieve our divine potential, change the world and, yes, glorify Him. We can do all those things if we surrender and follow Him.

# WEEK TWENTY SIX

SATURDAY/SUNDAY *God's Word*

## Facts of Life:

-Every book, chapter, and book of the Bible is God-breathed.

-The Holy Spirit will teach us what we need to know.

-God never changes, either does His Word.

Personal Reflections:

# WEEK TWENTY SEVEN

MONDAY *His Voice*

*Guard your steps when you go to the house of God.*
*To draw near to listen is better than to offer the sacrifice of fools,*
*for they do not know that they are doing evil.*
*Be not rash with your mouth, nor let your heart*
*be hasty to utter a word before God,*
*for God is in heaven and you are on earth.*
*Therefore let your words be few.*

Ecclesiastes 5:1-2

---

Um…it's obvious what King Solomon is saying here. His words should cause a bit of discomfort deep within our souls. Personally, I know I talk too much. I don't know why, I just do. It seems like there are many people in the world who have suffered from this same problem. But according to God it is more important for us to *"listen"* than talk. In His divine economy fewer words are better than many. We delude ourselves thinking we have so many good things to say. I wonder if we wouldn't be better off if we listened more instead of thinking we have so many significant things to say.

# WEEK TWENTY SEVEN

TUESDAY *His Voice*

*Moreover, he said to me,*
*"Son of man, all my words that I shall speak to you*
*receive in your heart,*
*and hear with your ears."*

Ezekiel 3:10

God speaks. He always has. He always will. He speaks to us in and through His Word, His Spirit, circumstances and the wise counsel of other Believers. But do we listen?

Our ears have been tickled for so long by human voices, our own thoughts and over stimulated by all that glitters in the world. That can make it hard to quiet our souls, listen, hear and recognize God's voice. He doesn't shout in order to be heard above the din that is our lives. He whispers, *"Come," "Be still"* and get to know Me (Psalm 46:10). The Bible promises that if we seek Him we will find Him and if we draw near to Him He will draw near to us (James 4:8). There's nothing more important than this.

# WEEK TWENTY SEVEN

WEDNESDAY *His Voice*

*But when you pray,*
*go into your room and shut the door*
*and pray to your Father who is in secret.*
*And your Father who sees in secret will reward you.*

Matthew 6:6

There are great and awesome treasures found when we seek Jesus and pray. He promises that if we obey and seek Him He will reveal Himself to us. That if we draw near to Him He will draw near to you and me. That's why He created us in the first place and the reason He died for our sin. When we do what He tells us to do He rewards our obedience. When we don't obey He can't. Sure, there will be times in our walk of faith that God may *feel* far away. But He's not. He promised that He would never leave or forsake us. We mean that much to Him. What better way is there to live life than devoting ourselves to seeking hard after Him?

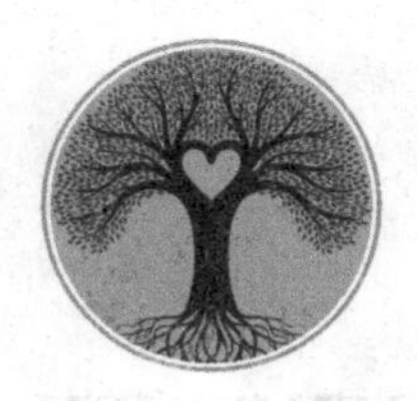

# WEEK TWENTY SEVEN

THURSDAY *His Voice*

*Nevertheless, I tell you the truth:*
*it is to your advantage that I go away,*
*for if I do not go away,*
*the Helper will not come to you.*
*But if I go, I will send him to you.*

John 16:7

---

"By enabling believers to actually receive this Spirit inside themselves, God initiated the most personal way He still speaks to us today – directly through the Holy Spirit, hand in hand with Scripture." Priscilla Shirer

It's amazing when you stop and think about it that Jesus came to earth for *our* sake. He climbed up on a cross and died a torturous and humiliating death for *our* sin. And when we accept Him as our personal Savior He sends His Spirit to live *in* us. The holy and perfect Son of God…His Spirit takes up residence in our souls. Could there be anything more mysterious and miraculous than this?

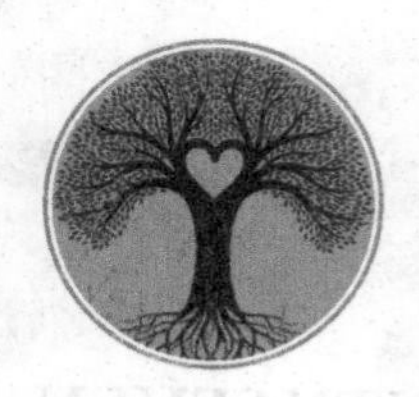

## WEEK TWENTY SEVEN

FRIDAY *His Voice*

*Do you not know that you are God's temple and that God's Spirit dwells in you?*

I Corinthians 3:16

The Holy Spirit of God lives in every believer's heart. That means that God is only a thought or a whisper away. And since the true purpose of life is to know, love and enjoy Him…in order for that to happen…some determination, intentionality and effort on our part is required.

Spending time with Jesus, studying His Word, praying and obeying…it's all about creating sacred space in our lives for Jesus. These acts of worship are a means of putting ourselves in a position to receive His love and love Him in turn.

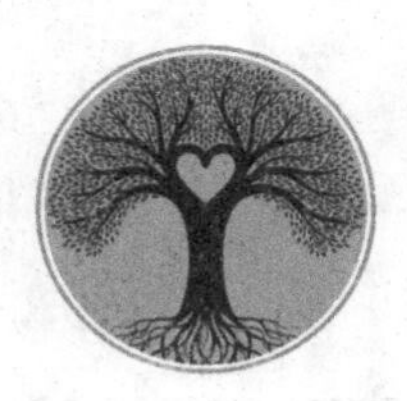

# WEEK TWENTY SEVEN

SATURDAY/SUNDAY *His Voice*

## Facts of Life:

-God is a communicative God.

-God still speaks to those who listens.

-True peace and hope are found in Him.

Personal Reflections:

# WEEK TWENTY EIGHT

MONDAY

## *Redeeming the Time*

*Look carefully then how you walk,*
*not as unwise but as wise,*
*making the best use of the time, because the days are evil.*

Ephesians 5:15-16

---

Life is a gift. A precious "gift" we did not deserve. God gave it to us anyway. Because of Him we have been blessed with the privilege of living life. Every day is important. Every minute matters. What we do with the next 24 hours – the thoughts we think, how we relate to one another…all of it will be noticed by God and have an impact on the world we live in. We are all valuable. We all have something important to contribute. That's why the apostle Paul warns us to be careful how we spend our time. We need to pay attention, make good choices and be aware of what we do with the gift of today we've been given. Everything matters to Him.

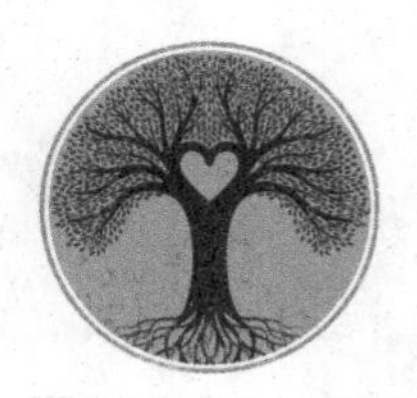

# WEEK TWENTY EIGHT

TUESDAY

## *Redeeming the Time*

*But do not overlook this one fact, beloved,*
*that with the Lord one day is as a thousand years,*
*and a thousand years as one day.*

II Peter 3:8

---

God is always working. He is doing everything that needs to be done. Plus He knows what He's doing and never runs out of time to accomplish *His* purpose. There are times when it feels like He's moving slowly – slow to answer our prayers, fix what is broken… mend our broken hearts. Then again, His ways are not our ways. His ways are perfect.

The Lord has a peculiar and methodical way of moving through our lives: loving, teaching, putting things right by a marvelous flow of continuous mercy and grace. Every minute of every day matters to God. Therefore, every day and every minute of every day must be handled with extreme care and love.

# WEEK TWENTY EIGHT

WEDNESDAY *Redeeming the Time*

Colossians 1:9-12

What does God want you to do with your life? Any idea? Well, finding the answer to that question is the key to living an abundant life.

First and foremost the Bible says that God created us to know Him personally, intimately and wants us to seek Him with all our hearts, with all our souls and with all our might. Knowing Him is the true purpose of life…to know, love and enjoy Him and be loved by Him. And, then, with the love we receive from Him we are able to love others.

With God's help we can do that, right? With God's help we can do anything.

# WEEK TWENTY EIGHT

THURSDAY

## *Redeeming the Time*

*Walk in wisdom toward outsiders,*
*making the best use of the time.*
*Let your speech always be gracious, seasoned with salt,*
*so that you may know how you ought to answer each person.*

Colossians 4:5-6

---

We may only have one chance to be kind to someone…to speak words of truth into their lives and introduce them to Jesus. Think about that. When you talk with someone it may be the only chance you will ever have to love and encourage them and explain to them what Jesus has done in life, not murmuring and complaining, but pouring into their souls words of light and hope.

Making moments with someone count for eternity has almost become a lost art.

# WEEK TWENTY EIGHT

FRIDAY *Redeeming the Time*

*For I know the plans I have for you,*
*declares the LORD, plans for welfare and not for evil,*
*to give you a future and a hope.*

Jeremiah 29:11

---

God cares and has a plan for our lives. I know that's a concept that is a little hard to wrap our minds around, but God cares and He cares deeply for each and every one of us. He wants to bless us with the fullness of Himself. We are His children. Why wouldn't He? He plans on drawing us closer and closer so we can enjoy His presence, experience His power and be transformed by His love.

The awe-inspiring mystery in all of this is that He made us and equipped us with everything we need to live the abundant life Jesus died to give us. If we're not doing that you got to ask yourself "Why not?"

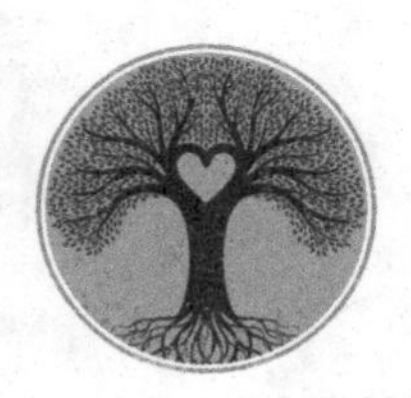

# WEEK TWENTY EIGHT

SATURDAY/SUNDAY *Redeeming the Time*

| Facts of Life: |
| --- |
| -Life is a gift. |
| -We have to be careful how we spend our time. |
| -Personally knowing God is the true purpose of life. |

Personal Reflections:

# WEEK TWENTY NINE

MONDAY *Kindness*

*Do nothing from selfish ambition or conceit,*
*but in humility count others more significant than yourselves.*
*Let each of you look not only to his own interests,*
*but also to the interests of others.*

Philippians 2:3-4

The statement of Paul's stands in direct contrast to what we see, hear and what is promoted in the world. That's because God's ways are not our ways. Humans look out for themselves. Self-absorption is the plague of the twenty first century. It started with Adam and Eve and it's been going downhill ever since. We are important and valuable to God. That is true. But we're not ALL important. We are not the only ones who are important to Him.

The take away from these verses is that one made in the image of God human being is as important as another. We all matter to God. Being kind and showing interest in someone else's life costs nothing. And when we are kind to someone today, who knows, someone just may be kind to us tomorrow.

# WEEK TWENTY NINE

TUESDAY *Kindness*

*Render true judgments,*
*show kindness and mercy to one another,*
*do not oppress the widow, the fatherless,*
*the sojourner, or the poor,*
*and let none of you devise evil against another in your heart.*

Zechariah 7:9-10

---

The prophet Zechariah understood the importance of kindness. He knew that random acts of kindness could improve the human condition and change the world.

Basically there are two kinds of people: *self-absorbed takers* and *others-oriented givers.* By virtue of our mindset and attitude we align ourselves with one or the other. The "self-absorbed takers" inhabit an unhealthy community of one. The "others oriented givers" world is infinite and filled with people of all different shapes and sizes, ethnic backgrounds, colors and creeds. Those who are givers enjoy opportunities to love others, demonstrate kindness and give their lives away for the pleasure and glory of Jesus Christ. And that's the way things are supposed to be

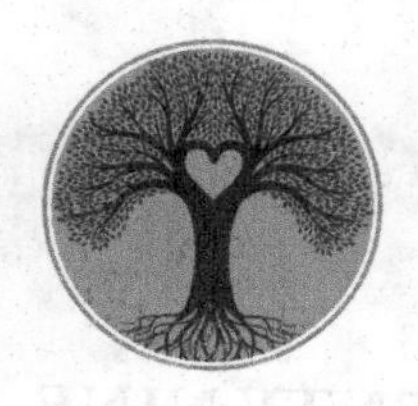

# WEEK TWENTY NINE

WEDNESDAY

*Kindness*

*In all things I have shown you that by working hard*
*in this way we must help the weak*
*and remember the words of the Lord Jesus,*
*how he himself said,*
*"It is more blessed to give than to receive."*

Acts 20:35

We've all been hurt, abused, betrayed and disappointed by life in one way or another, at one time or another. It goes along with being human and living in a fallen world. At the same time, we have what it takes to move beyond ourselves, have compassion and help others who are trying to find their way in a hurting world.

Jesus smiles when we give our lives away. What's ultimately important is that we use what He gave us to bless others. That's the way He intended us to live. It's not necessarily important "what" we do for the good of others but that we "do" something. Every small act of kindness helps.

# WEEK TWENTY NINE

THURSDAY

*Kindness*

*Rejoice with those who rejoice,*
*weep with those who weep.*

Romans 12:15

---

We'd rather laugh than cry with someone, right? It can be uncomfortable engaging with someone who is in crisis and suffering. That doesn't mean we shouldn't go there.

Laughing and crying with one another is important. It brings and binds people together, and we need both. It's important to know that someone will be "there" for us…ready and willing to rejoice when we rejoice, yes, but also weep with us when we cry. Once we get past the caring only about ourselves bit…things get easier. King Solomon said that "Two are better than one." And he is one hundred percent correct.

# WEEK TWENTY NINE

FRIDAY *Kindness*

*Be kind to one another, tenderhearted,*
*forgiving one another, as God in Christ forgave you.*

Ephesians 4:32

Forgiveness is the greatest act of kindness. It's not always easy, but it liberates our souls. Forgiveness is a choice, really. A "choice" we may have to make one or more times every day. God forgave us. We forgive others. It's part of the ebb and flow of living a healthy God-honoring life.

Yes, we can hang on to grievances and bitterness and play the martyr. But a lack of charity will destroy us from the inside out. And why would we do that to ourselves when we can forgive and let God's grace flow into and, then, through our lives?

## WEEK TWENTY NINE

SATURDAY/SUNDAY *Kindness*

Facts of Life:

-Be interested in others.

-Being kind changes the world.

-Forgiveness matters.

Personal Reflections:

# WEEK THIRTY

MONDAY

*Trust*

*Trust in the LORD with all your heart,*
*and do not lean on your own understanding.*
*In all your ways acknowledge him,*
*and he will make straight your paths.*

Proverbs 3:5-6

---

God knows everything: past, present and future. He is intimately aware of who we are and what we're not. He made us, understands what we're going through here and now, tomorrow and forever. On top of all that He wants the best for us and intends to work everything in our lives together for our ultimate good.

Our job is to trust Him. We may not know exactly where we're going or what we're doing and what's happening around us, but He does. We may not be able to trust others and, reality is, often we can't. But we can trust God. He's on our side and is constantly working to lead us into the abundant life.

## WEEK THIRTY

TUESDAY *Trust*

*Blessed is the man who makes*
*the Lord his trust,*
*who does not turn to the proud,*
*to those who go astray after a lie!*

Psalm 40:4

---

God abundantly blesses those who trust Him. He is able to actively participate in our lives and prove that He *is* God when we lean in and rely on Him. When we're self-sufficiently…we're bound to be disappointed. When we put our trust in other people…we will often be disappointed. People are finite creatures, just like we are. World systems and institutions are run by created beings and, therefore, they'll let us down as well. But God…Never!

He *can* be trusted. Nothing is impossible with Him.

## WEEK THIRTY

WEDNESDAY *Trust*

*So that they should set their hope in God*
*and not forget the works of God,*
*but keep his commandments.*

Psalm 78:7

---

Asaph, the inspired author of Psalm 78, is instructing us instructing us in the art of living. We are to trust God and put our confidence in Him. It is essential that we live surrendered lives and allow God to actively participate in our lives, not just when we're in a bind with our backs against a wall, but every day, today, tomorrow and for the rest of our lives. Enjoying Jesus as our partner in life is what He created us for.

No. It isn't easy learning how to relate to God in this partnership sort of way, but it *is* possible. And besides - It's the only thing that truly satisfies the deepest longings of our souls.

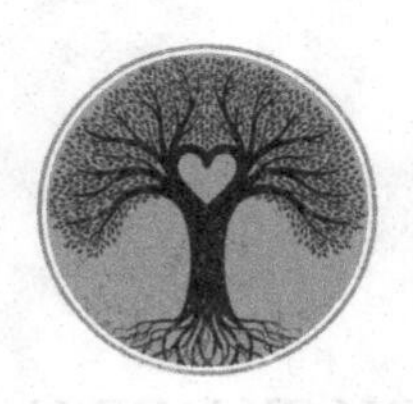

# WEEK THIRTY

THURSDAY

*Trust*

*Every word of God proves true;*
*he is a shield to those who take refuge in him.*

Proverbs 30:5

---

The world can be a confusing and dangerous place. That's why God invites us to take refuge in Him. He is available morning, noon, and night, 24/7, today and every day. And He always will be. But taking *refuge* in God's presence isn't just about hiding from life. It's about finding comfort, encouragement, and courage to live as He would have us live…learning how to love as He loves and tapping into His wisdom and grace so we can change the world for His glory.

Spending time in the presence of God can be a humbling experience. But it's also a powerful reminder that we are not alone.

## WEEK THIRTY

FRIDAY *Trust*

*Therefore, since we have been justified by faith,*
*we have peace with God through our Lord Jesus Christ.*

Romans 5:1

Living a life of faith begins when we accept Jesus as our personal Savior. From that point on, as we study His Word and experience His love, we learn that He is faithful and that He knows what He's doing and can be trusted. As a result our faith grows. By faith we are saved, justified and reconciled to God. And by faith we live our lives *for* and *with* Him.

By an intentional act of our wills we choose to believe that He is who He says He is and that He will do everything He promised. Faith isn't just an ethereal ideal or archaic concept. It is *the* most powerful, safe and practical way to live life.

## WEEK THIRTY

SATURDAY/SUNDAY

Facts of Life:

-Trusting God leads to abundant living.

-God can be trusted.

-God is willing to help.

Personal Reflections:

# WEEK THIRTY ONE

MONDAY *Authenticity*

Psalm 139:13-17

There is a sweet something special that happens deep in our souls when we embrace our God-given identity and celebrate the "who" He created us to be. It changes things when we realize that we were handmade by God and that we are who we are for a divinely appointed reason. The Lord our God is intimately aware of every fiber of our being. He has numbered every hair on our heads. He knows our thoughts and understands precisely who and what we are and what we are not. He made us! Why wouldn't He?

It pleases our heavenly Father when we enjoy being the person He intended us to be. After all, He made us and we do belong to Him.

# WEEK THIRTY ONE

TUESDAY *Authenticity*

*So God created man in his own image,*
*in the image of God he created him;*
*male and female he created them.*

Genesis 1:27

You were personally and deliberately created in the image of God. You did *not* evolve from some puddle of goo. God wanted YOU! He made YOU! In His eyes you are an unfinished work of art. And because the idea of you originated in the heart of God, finding your true identity in Christ is one of the most important things you will ever do.

Everyone has issues and things they struggle with. No one's life is perfect. But by the power of God working in us issues can be dealt with, managed successfully and resolved. Yes, you *are* a handmade work of art in God's eyes. That's true, but there's still a bit of polishing He wants to do.

# WEEK THIRTY ONE

WEDNESDAY *Authenticity*

*You did not choose me,*
*but I chose you and appointed you*
*that you should go and bear fruit and that your fruit should abide,*
*so that whatever you ask the Father in my name,*
*he may give it to you.*

John 15:16

The fact that God wanted us, made us and that we belong to Him can be a bit overwhelming and a huge encouragement at the same time. We belong to God. Can you imagine? That means that the Great Big God of the Universe will help us achieve our divine potential and has promised to finish the work He started in us.

God can heal our brokenness and reform our thinking. He can make us over into the people He wants and needs us to be. He blessed us with all sorts of talents, strengths and abilities when He formed us in our mother's womb and has great things He wants to do *in* us and *through* us. Think of what our lives would look like if we let Him.

# WEEK THIRTY ONE

THURSDAY *Authenticity*

*I praise you, for I am fearfully and wonderfully made.*
*Wonderful are your works;*
*my soul knows it very well.*
*My frame was not hidden from you,*
*when I was being made in secret,*
*intricately woven in the depths of the earth.*

Psalm 139:14-15

---

We were handmade by God. Have you ever stopped to think about how absolutely amazing that is? It changes things. The Lord and Creator of the whole world wove every fiber of our being together deliberately and personally. He made us the way we are, hand-picked the talents, strengths and abilities we have and designed our spirits in a specific way so we could enjoy and love and serve Him.

It's humbling to know the investment God made to make us who we are. He has plans for our lives. He wants us to succeed and be true to our God-given identity. Besides…being inauthentic never works and is exhausting.

# WEEK THIRTY ONE

FRIDAY

*Authenticity*

*Before I formed you in the womb I knew you,*
*and before you were born I consecrated you;*
*I appointed you a prophet to the nations.*

Jeremiah 1:5

---

God had a plan about *who* we would be and *what* we would do before He made us. His plan was specific as well as personalized. He lovingly created us because He wanted us and built into us the strengths, abilities and talents…the sense of humor, or lack thereof, emotional make up and disposition that He wanted us to have so we could accomplish His purposes. We have what we need to be the person He intended us to be. We can improve the human condition and change our world if we let Him have His way.

The key to this success story of course is to be true to our God-given identity and obey.

# WEEK THIRTY ONE

SATURDAY/SUNDAY

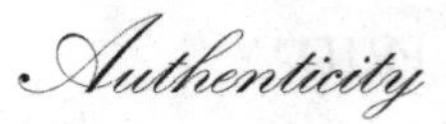


Facts of Life:

-We are who we are for a reason.

-God wanted us, made us. We belong to Him.

-We are who we are because of God's creative genius and grand design.

Personal Reflections:

# WEEK THIRTY TWO

MONDAY

*God's Will*

*You shall love the LORD your God*
*with all your heart and with all your soul*
*and with all your might.*

Deuteronomy 6:5

God wanted and loved us before we were even born. He sent His Son to die for our sin so we could escape hell, spend eternity in heaven with Him and live an abundant life. How mysterious and divinely magical it is to be loved by God. Loving Him with our whole heart is the least we can do to demonstrate our appreciation for all He's done.

Since God created us and saves our souls, it just makes sense that we should be grateful. God deserves our love more than anyone in heaven or down here on earth. And, besides, when loving our God is our number one priority…we are fulfilled, happy and blest.

## WEEK THIRTY TWO

TUESDAY *God's Will*

*This is my commandment,*
*that you love one another as I have loved you.*

John 15:12

John 15:17 is a command, not a request. God is letting us know what His perfect will is for our lives and, at the same time, He reveals the desire of His heart. Loving one another is important to Him. And the key to loving others, really, is to surrender our wills and obey Him. Obedience is a choice we have to make pretty much every minute of every day that we live. When we choose to obey God…His Spirit teaches us what true love looks like, sounds like, and how it behaves.

Jesus came to earth to die for our sin. He is our perfect example of what it looks like to die to self and give our lives away.

# WEEK THIRTY TWO

WEDNESDAY

*God's Will*

*Make me to know your ways, O Lord;*
*teach me your paths.*
*Lead me in your truth and teach me,*
*for you are the God of my salvation;*
*for you I wait all the day long.*

Psalm 25:4-5

---

We are supposed to *wait* on God today, tomorrow and every day for the rest of our lives. The word "wait" in the original Hebrew language doesn't refer to passivity, a do nothing posture of total disengagement and rest. Instead, it carries with it the idea of working hard to bind ourselves to God as we *wait* on Him to answer our prayers, direct our steps and give us the courage and strength to obey Him. Our job is to seek God in the "waiting" and put our trust in Him.

Yes, life is a challenge. And we're only finite human beings, which puts us at a huge disadvantage. Let's face it there's no possible way we can handle life on our own. But with God's help we can do anything.

# WEEK THIRTY TWO

THURSDAY *God's Will*

*Only be very careful to observe the commandment*
*and the law that Moses the servant of the LORD commanded you,*
*to love the LORD your God,*
*and to walk in all his ways and to keep his commandments*
*and to cling to him*
*and to serve him with all your heart and with all your soul.*

Joshua 22:5

---

What a privilege it is to know and serve Jesus. He gave us life. He saves our souls. He blesses us with abundance. His goodness and extravagant generosity exceeds human comprehension.

However, Christianity isn't just about believing in Jesus and escaping hell. It's about serving Him and using the talents, abilities and equipment He gave us to accomplish His purposes here on earth. So we fix our eyes on Jesus and surrender our lives to Him. In turn, He invites us to join Him in the work He's doing on earth and we accept. What a simple and easy way to live life.

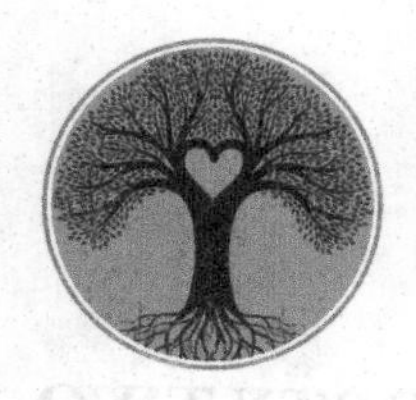

## WEEK THIRTY TWO

FRIDAY *God's Will*

*Have this mind among yourselves, which is yours in Christ Jesus,*
*who, though he was in the form of God,*
*did not count equality with God a thing to be grasped,*
*but emptied himself, by taking the form of a servant,*
*being born in the likeness of men.*
*And being found in human form,*
*he humbled himself by becoming obedient to the point of death,*
*even death on a cross.*

Philippians 2:5-8

---

Jesus died to save us from ourselves and give us abundant life. Contemporary society promotes the erroneous notion that *our* reputation, *our* will, *our* comfort and *our* success is more important than anything, even God's purpose for our lives. That's absurd. It's not!

We're not more important than God. We wouldn't even exist if it weren't for Him. We'd end up spending eternity in hell if He hadn't died for our sin. We owe Jesus everything. He was the King of Kings and, yet, He humbled Himself and became a servant. Now it's our turn to do the exact same thing.

## WEEK THIRTY TWO

SATURDAY/SUNDAY

*God's Will*

### Facts of Life:

-Loving others is important to God.

-Jesus gave His life so we might live.

-Jesus served. Now we get to serve and be like Him.

Personal Reflections:

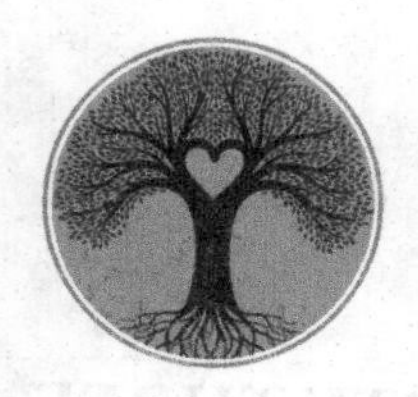

# WEEK THIRTY THREE

MONDAY

*Worry*

*Do not be anxious about anything,*
*but in everything by prayer and supplication with thanksgiving*
*let your requests be made known to God.*
*And the peace of God, which surpasses all understanding,*
*will guard your hearts and your minds in Christ Jesus.*

Philippians 4:6-7

Worry doesn't just happen. We allow it to happen. It accomplishes nothing and can have an adverse effect on our minds, bodies and even our souls. But all that bad stuff can be avoided if we lean in God's direction and share our concerns with Him. He cares. When we pray and cry out for His help He listens. He listens not only to our petitions but He's ready and willing to get involved, carry our burdens and help.

Our heavenly Father never intended for us to worry, about anything. It's not good for us. He's there for us. He wants us to confide in Him and trust Him. And He can be trusted. That's something we all have to learn.

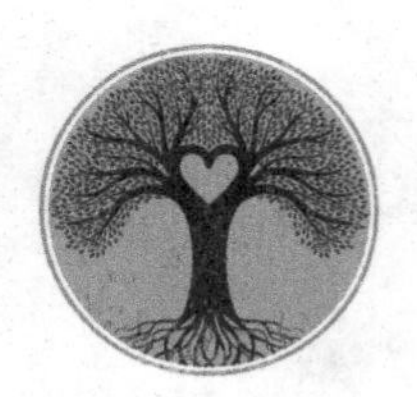

# WEEK THIRTY THREE

TUESDAY *Worry*

Matthew 6:25-33

Something divinely magical happens when we step out of worry into trust. It requires an intentional decision on our part…a decision to take God at His Word and rest in His loving embrace. He knows what we need better than we do. When we humble ourselves and trust Him the burdens we carry become light and in His presence we find divine power, relief and hope.

It's always a good thing when we talk to Jesus about our fears, needs and problems. After all, the One who owns everything in heaven and on earth has shared all He possesses with us. Because of His generosity we lack nothing.

## WEEK THIRTY THREE

WEDNESDAY *Worry*

*Therefore do not be anxious about tomorrow,*
*for tomorrow will be anxious for itself.*
*Sufficient for the day is its own trouble.*

Matthew 6:34

The key to living a worry free life is to keep our eyes on Jesus. Freedom from worry. Isn't that what it comes down to and what we all want from life. If we want financial wealth and material possessions we can spend our lives striving after those things. But if we want *true* abundance...the peace we long for and desperately need... spiritual freedom, contentment and joy...then we have to shift our focus. We must stop striving after the things of earth and seek Jesus with all our heart, soul and might.

He's waiting patiently to bless us with everything we long for and truly need. All good things are found in the personal knowledge of Him.

# WEEK THIRTY THREE

THURSDAY

*Worry*

Luke 12:22-31

This is a command, not a request. Worry is hazardous to our emotional stability and our physical and spiritual health. So Jesus tells us not to worry and assures us that He will take care of our lives.

So how *do* we handle the pressures of life? By turning to Jesus. By seeking Jesus, deliberately and spending quality time with Him every day. We meditate on His Word and think about *who* He is and how much He loves us. We put our faith in Him and hold on to the fact that nothing is impossible with Him. He never leaves or abandons us. He never makes us go-it-alone when it comes to dealing with life's challenges. He wants to take care of us. We just have to let Him.

# WEEK THIRTY THREE

FRIDAY *Worry*

*Trust in the* L*ORD* *with all your heart,*
*and do not lean on your own understanding.*
*In all your ways acknowledge him,*
*and he will make straight your paths.*

Proverbs 3:5-6

---

Proverbs 3:5-6 seems to conjure up an image of a nun lying face down at an altar surrendering her life to Jesus. "Surrender" is all about acknowledging that Jesus *is* God and that He can be trusted.

The world insists that self-sufficiency is the highest form of success and that being in control of everyone and everything is what we all should aspire to. But from God's perspective success is all about surrender and following Him. He has a plan for our success and wants to bless us with insight, wisdom, divine power and do for us what we cannot do for ourselves.

## WEEK THIRTY THREE

SATURDAY/SUNDAY

Facts of Life:

-Worry accomplishes nothing.

-We are blessed when we step out of worry into trust.

-God will work everything together
for our God, if we let Him.

Personal Reflections:

# WEEK THIRTY FOUR

MONDAY

*Humility*

*Have this mind among yourselves, which is yours in Christ Jesus,*
*who, though he was in the form of God,*
*did not count equality with God a thing to be grasped,*
*but emptied himself, by taking the form of a servant,*
*being born in the likeness of men.*
*And being found in human form,*
*he humbled himself by becoming obedient to the point of death,*
*even death on a cross.*

Philippians 2:5-8

---

What a beautiful picture of the humility and humanity of Jesus Christ. He was fully God and, at the same time, fully human. And being perfect and sinless, He was the one and only person who could die and pay the price for our sin and save our souls from hell. So He did, voluntarily.

Looking at and meditating on the sacrifice Jesus made on our behalf should inspire us…make us want to walk in His footsteps, follow His example and learn to be more like Him. That won't be easy. But it *is* doable. Fixing our eyes on Jesus is the key.

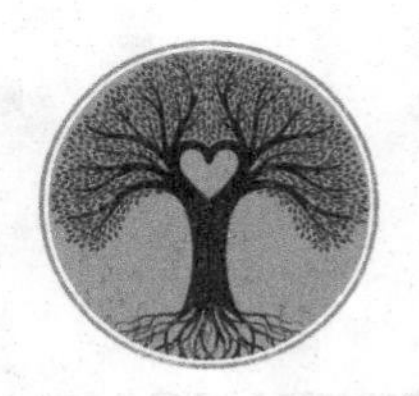

# WEEK THIRTY FOUR

TUESDAY *Humility*

*Humble yourselves, therefore,*
*under the mighty hand of God*
*so that at the proper time he may exalt you.*

I Peter 5:6

---

God is…well, God. We're only human. The world promotes the erroneous notion that if we try hard enough we can become gods. It's a stupid notion. Nothing could be further from the truth, and we can't.

We are feeble, frail, sin-ridden human beings, certainly not God material in the least. Granted, we do have potential. But that "potential" is based on God's grace and supernatural power working in us. We can do nothing of true and lasting value on our own. But if we surrender our lives to Jesus and let Him have His way in us – we can do some pretty amazing things. We can love the unlovable, care for the needy, lead people to Christ and, yes, even change the world.

# WEEK THIRTY FOUR

WEDNESDAY *Humility*

*But the meek shall inherit the land*
*and delight themselves in abundant peace.*

Psalm 37:11

---

I am not promoting what is currently called "The Prosperity Gospel." Jesus' followers have problems just like everyone else. We live in a fallen world that's filled with imperfect people. We're bound to have problems, face trials and we will always will. But what King David is explaining in this psalm is that if we are humble and flexible in God's hands, we will enjoy God's peace and experience His prosperity in spite of it all.

It all comes down to cultivating intimacy with Jesus, really. He is the Prince of Peace and knowing Him should be our highest aspiration and goal. So we seek Him and learn the truth about Him...put our trust in Him. Knowing Jesus personally and intimately is where true prosperity is found.

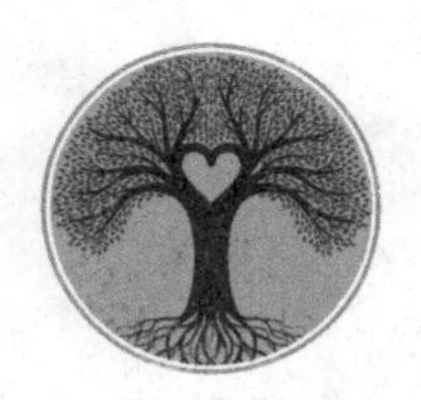

# WEEK THIRTY FOUR

THURSDAY *Humility*

*When pride comes, then comes disgrace,*
*but with the humble is wisdom.*

Proverbs 11:2

---

We *think* that we know-it-all. But compared to God we know nothing and understand even less. We inherited Adam's predisposition to think more highly of ourselves than we should. And we're stubborn on top of everything else. But there is a solution to our problem.

It starts when we admit that God *is* God and He knows more than we do. Then, when we recognize and admit that, God's Spirit is free to teach us the divine truths we don't know. That's when life gets really interesting. If we are wise we will make it our business to listen to what God has to say and learn from Him. Sure, we can continue to stumble through life armed only with human logic and wisdom. But with His divine truth at our disposal why would we?

# WEEK THIRTY FOUR

FRIDAY

*Humility*

*One who is wise is cautious and turns away from evil,*
*but a fool is reckless and careless.*

Proverbs 14:16

King Solomon is giving us some good advice here. There's a huge difference between living life according to God's wisdom and ignoring Him. The interesting thing is - God never intended for us to live life on our own. He intended on being our partner for life. He leads. We follow. He speaks. We listen and obey. His way is simple, and it works.

Success isn't about plotting our own course, being in control and making things happen for ourselves. God created life and has a plan for each one of us. He wants the best for us. Our success will depend on whether or not we surrender and follow Him.

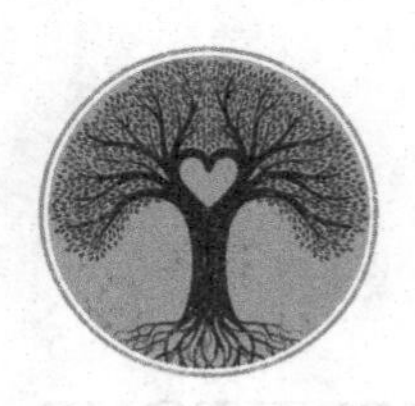

# WEEK THIRTY FOUR

SATURDAY/SUNDAY

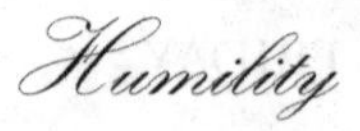


## Facts of Life:

-Jesus humbled Himself and voluntarily died for our sin.

-God is God. We're only human.

-God knows it all, we only think we do.

Personal Reflections:

# WEEK THIRTY FIVE

MONDAY

*Contentment*

*I can do all things*
*through him who strengthens me.*

Philippians 4:13

---

According to the Bible contentment is not necessarily something we're born with. God gave Adam and Eve every good and perfect gift and they weren't satisfied. Sadly, we inherited our dissatisfaction and ingratitude from them.

Think about it! Adam and Eve had everything they needed to thrive and enjoy life, but they wanted more and their rebellion cost them everything.

Contentment is a learned phenomenon, really, a special grace that we receive from God when we walk closely with Him. It's a matter of exchanging our wills for the will of God and appreciating His extravagant generosity.

# WEEK THIRTY FIVE

TUESDAY *Contentment*

*Keep your life free from love of money,*
*and be content with what you have,*
*for he has said, "I will never leave you nor forsake you."*

Hebrews 13:5

Jesus is *with* us, in the most personal, loving and eternal sense. It is His presence in our lives that makes life worth living. That is why the enemy tries to rob us of the joy that knowing Jesus intimately brings. The things of *this* earth are not the true treasures of life. Knowing, loving and enjoying Jesus is.

Yes, we have to earn a living, provide for our families and be responsible. But the sum total of our portfolio and bank account and what we can acquire and possess shouldn't shouldn't be the main focus of our attention. Jesus is.

The truth of the matter is - Contentment and joy comes to those who know and love Jesus with their whole heart.

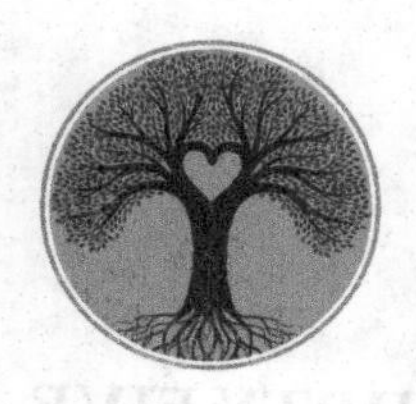

# WEEK THIRTY FIVE

WEDNESDAY

*Contentment*

*For the sake of Christ, then, I am content with weaknesses, insults, hardships, persecutions, and calamities. For when I am weak, then I am strong.*

II Corinthians 12:10

The Apostle Paul pretty much covers all the "negatives" we may face on planet earth. We will all experience trials and tribulations, insults and have to endure hardships. Many of us will even be persecuted from time to time. These things are bound to happen. We live in a mixed up, corrupt and fallen world. Our heavenly Father is trying to educate and warn us…prepare us for what is bound to happen to all of us at one point in our lives or another. It helps to be forewarned. At least then we can prepare ourselves for the inevitable and stick like glue to Jesus where we will find courage and strength in Him.

## WEEK THIRTY FIVE

THURSDAY *Contentment*

Deuteronomy 7:7-9

Jesus has done many great things for us. What could be more unexpected and extraordinary than Him dying on a cross for our sin? What could possibly be more unlikely than the Son of God sending His Spirit to live in us to teach us about life, guide our steps and pour supernatural life into our dead souls?

In a world where there are so many lies running rampant…so much negativity, pessimism and fear…it is vitally important for us to stay connected to Jesus, read our Bibles and fill our hearts and minds with what is true. Cultivating intimacy with Jesus helps us focus on the hope of heaven and shields us from all the bad stuff that's happening here on earth. He longs to love on us and make the fullness of His love and glory known.

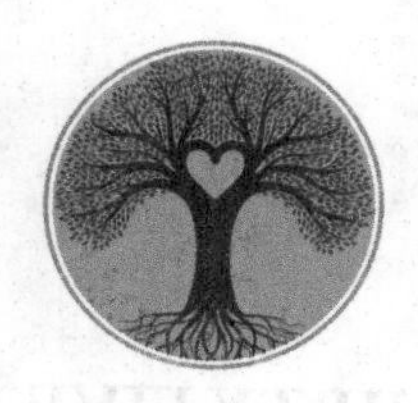

# WEEK THIRTY FIVE

FRIDAY *Contentment*

*For the sake of Christ, then,*
*I am content with weaknesses, insults,*
*hardships, persecutions, and calamities.*
*For when I am weak, then I am strong.*

II Corinthians 12:10

---

God will lead us, if we let Him. He led two million Israelites out of Egypt and delivered them from slavery. He has every intention of leading us too. He's been trying to lead His children through life and getting them out of trouble for generations. You'd think that after thousands and thousands of years He'd be tired of dealing with a bunch of stubborn, stiff-necked children…dusting them off and getting them lined out and headed in the right direction again and again and AGAIN! But our heavenly Father is loving, faithful and relentless. He never gives up on those who belong to Him…NEVER! even when we give up on ourselves.

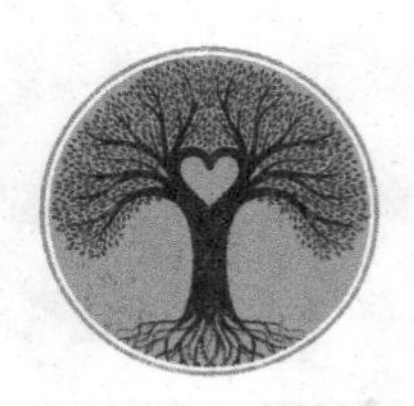

## WEEK THIRTY FIVE

SATURDAY/SUNDAY

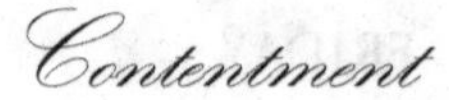


### Facts of Life:

-Contentment is a learned phenomenon.

-We are weak. God is strong.

-Knowing Jesus intimately is the prize.

Personal Reflections:

# WEEK THIRTY SIX

MONDAY

## *God's Power*

Genesis 1

God created the heavens and the earth and…well, everything. And He created it with a word. He also made you and me. It's all so amazing, but still true. The incomprehensibility of God's creative power is hard to wrap our minds around. So much of who He is and what He does is beyond human comprehension. But our inability to understand doesn't make the facts about God less true. He said, "Let there be light" and there was light. He said, "Let us make man in. Our image" and He did. God isn't limited by time, space or human limitations. He's God. His very nature is surrounded in mystery. So instead of struggling to understand why not accept His glory by faith and enjoy Him?

# WEEK THIRTY SIX

TUESDAY

*God's Power*

For to be sure, he was crucified in weakness,
yet he lives by God's power. Likewise, we are weak in him,
yet by God's power we will live with
him in our dealing with you.

II Corinthians 13:4

---

The power Jesus used to raise Himself from the dead is now at work in those who believe. Nothing is impossible for Him therefore nothing is impossible for you and for me.

Yes, there are times when life gets hard and confusing. But God is still God and Jesus' power is still at work. Absolutely, things do happen that we can't deal with, figure out or control. Jesus is still working. He never quits. He never takes a day off or abandons us. His job is to work everything in our lives, even what we perceive to be the bad stuff, together for our ultimate good. Our job is to trust in Him.

# WEEK THIRTY SIX

WEDNESDAY

*God's Power*

*My grace is sufficient for you,*
*for my power is made perfect in weakness.*

II Corinthians 12:9

---

We are weak. On the other hand God is scary strong. We are finite and limited. God is not. Life can be challenging. Absolutely! We live in a fallen world. We're sinners and apart from Jesus we can't do much of anything. But *with* Him? Now that's another story entirely.

We're not alone. Jesus is always with us and is willing to fight our battles for us and do whatever needs to be done. Besides all that He has great plans for us. He is prepared to give us a future and provide us with hope. The real mystery is that He wants to use us to love people out of brokenness and change the world. He can. We never will.

# WEEK THIRTY SIX

THURSDAY

*God's Power*

Philippians 4:11-13

The apostle Paul wasn't exactly the healthiest guy. He suffered physical problems and endured a lot of pain over the years. So he prayed. He prayed and asked God to heal him. But for whatever reason God said, "No."

The divine magic in this story is that in spite of all his suffering Paul authored over half the New Testament, planted churches, preached the gospel message here, there and everywhere and led people to Jesus Christ. And in spite of being persecuted, physically tortured and facing heinous hardships, he learned to be content. Um...if Paul did we can too.

## WEEK THIRTY SIX

FRIDAY

*God's Power*

Joshua 6:1-25

Is this a true story? Yes. Yes, it is. Jericho wasn't taken and destroyed by what one would call "normal" strategic acumen and military might. The city was taken and overthrown by God's divine and supernatural power. That's the whole point of the story and what He wants us to learn about Him.

At this particular point in human history God's chosen people had just entered the Promised Land after wandering through the desert for forty years because of their unbelief. They lacked faith and had rebelled against God over and over again. They needed to know that God was exactly who He had declared Himself to be. That's why the Lord orchestrated this rather bazaar and, at the same time, humorous scenario to prove it. And…as the saying goes…the rest is history.

# WEEK THIRTY SIX

SATURDAY/SUNDAY

Facts of Life:

-Everything God says about Himself is true.

-Nothing is impossible with God.

-Jesus raised Himself from the grave and that same power is at work in you and me.

Personal Reflections:

# WEEK THIRTY SEVEN

MONDAY

*Forgiveness*

*And no longer shall each one teach his neighbor*
*and each his brother, saying,*
*"Know the LORD,"*
*for they shall all know me,*
*from the least of them to the greatest,*
*declares the LORD.*
*For I will forgive their iniquity,*
*and I will remember their sin no more.*

Jeremiah 31:34

Jesus is our example of how to love, think and live. That means we have a special Someone, the best possible "Someone," that we can look up to, imitate and trust. When you stop and think about it He has all sorts of reasons why He should hold grudges against us, but He doesn't. He showers us with mercy instead. We tend to be mean spirited, self-centered complainers. The Lord has compassion, loves unconditionally and sympathizes with our man weaknesses. We deserve hell. He forgives, showers us with mercy and gifts us with heaven instead.

# WEEK THIRTY SEVEN

TUESDAY *Forgiveness*

*For you, O Lord, are good and forgiving,*
*abounding in steadfast love to all who call upon you.*

Psalm 86:5

The Great and Awesome God of the Universe loves us and forgives our sin. What more could we ask for or want?

The Lord's infinite capacity to love and forgive us is difficult to comprehend. We get mad and hold grudges. He does not. Our love is conditional. It runs hot one day and cold the next…here today and gone tomorrow. But God? His love is unconditional, tenacious, relentless and He never gives up. He loved us before we were born. He loves us today. He will love us tomorrow and go right on loving us until the day we die…even after. His steadfast love is a gift. Humble gratitude should be our response.

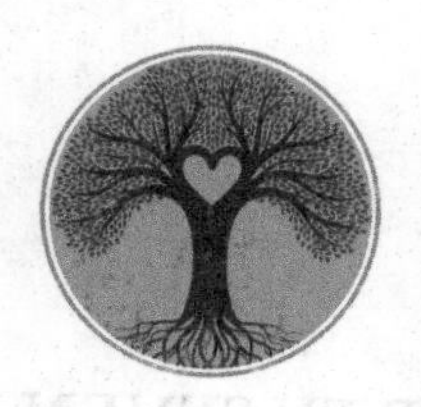

## WEEK THIRTY SEVEN

WEDNESDAY

*Forgiveness*

*If we confess our sins,*
*he is faithful and just to forgive us our sins*
*and to cleanse us from all unrighteousness.*

I John 1:9|

We've all done things we're ashamed of: lied, cheated, turned our backs on God, rebelled and disobeyed. But He's willing to forgive our sin if we ask Him to.

Sin separates us from God. That's the horrible thing. It creates a wall between Him and you and Him and me…makes enjoying our relationship with Him complicated. And on top of all that… sin robs us of spiritual health and the abundant life Christ died to give us. So why wouldn't we go to our Father and confess our sin to Him, which is, simply, agreeing with Him that what we did was wrong? Think about it – He's with us and knows about it anyway.

# WEEK THIRTY SEVEN

THURSDAY *Forgiveness*

*And do not grieve the Holy Spirit of God,*
*by whom you were sealed for the day of redemption.*
*Let all bitterness and wrath and anger*
*and clamor and slander be put away from you,*
*along with all malice.*
*Be kind to one another, tenderhearted,*
*forgiving one another, as God in Christ forgave you.*

Ephesians 4:30-32

---

We are supposed to forgive others the way God forgives us. It makes Him happy. It's surprising to think that we have it within our power to please God and make Him smile. Or, conversely, we can disappoint and make Him weep by our behavior.

We tend to forget that our choices, big or small, make a difference to God. He's with us and notices everything. He knows whether we love or hate…whether we forgive or hold grudges…treat people with kindness or are cruel. Our every thought, word, even the intentions of our hearts affects our Biggest Fan and Forever Friend. Keep that in mind…He notices and knows everything.

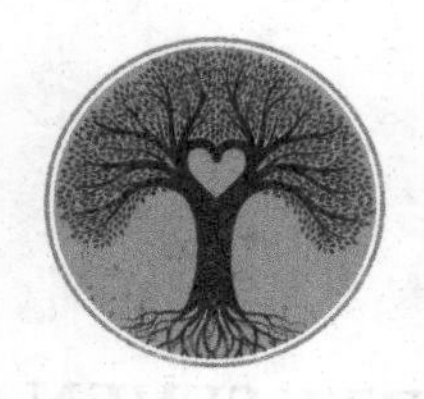

# WEEK THIRTY SEVEN

FRIDAY

*Forgiveness*

*Then Peter came up and said to him,*
*"Lord, how often will my brother sin against me,*
*and I forgive him? As many as seven times?"*
*Jesus said to him,*
*"I do not say to you seven times,*
*but seventy-seven times."*

Matthew 18:21-22

---

God's standards are high. He explains in His Word that we are a *"royal priesthood"* and a *"chosen generation."* He also says that we are *to be holy as He is holy* and He never asks us to do anything that we cannot do with His help – including forgiving others as He forgives us.

After telling us to forgive each other seven times seventy if necessary, the Lord will, then, provide us with the grace and divine power we need to obey. We may be weak, unsure and unable. But He is strong and can do anything in, with and through us if we let Him. Hallelujah, Amen.

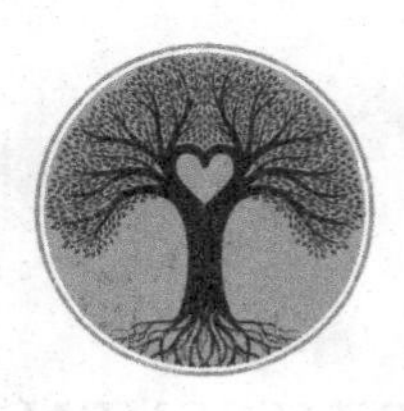

# WEEK THIRTY SEVEN

SATURDAY/SUNDAY *Forgiveness*

## Facts of Life:

-When we confess our sin, God will forgive us.

-God smiles when we forgive.

-God forgives and by His power
working in us we can forgive.

Personal Reflections:

# WEEK THIRTY EIGHT

MONDAY

*Selflessness*

Philippians 2:5-8

---

If we want to learn and spiritually grow and be all we can be... we have to adopt Christ's mindset and attitude as our own. He surrendered and embraced His Father's will. He came to earth, died for our sin and cared more about *our* well-being than His own.

Contrary to what most people think and believe, life isn't just about us. Yes, every individual is valuable to God, regardless of their political persuasion, ethnicity or the color of their skin. And, because we all matter to God we should humble ourselves, love one another the way He loves and give our lives away for the good of all and God's glory.

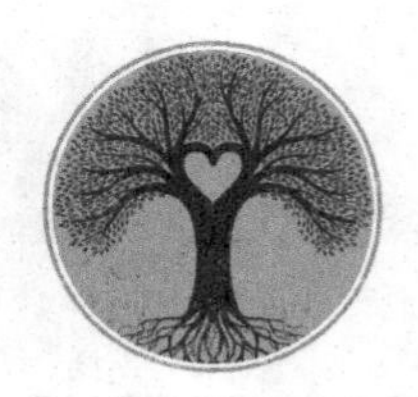

## WEEK THIRTY EIGHT

TUESDAY *Selflessness*

*For you know the grace of our Lord Jesus Christ,*
*that though he was rich, yet for your sake he became poor,*
*so that you by his poverty might become rich.*

II Corinthians 8:9

Jesus epitomizes the art of *selflessness.* He reigned in heaven and had supreme authority over everyone and everything. Still, because He cared so deeply about those He created, He came to earth and died for our sin so we could live forever in heaven with Him. He volunteered to do for us what we could not possibly do for ourselves. That's how perfectly He loves. He gave up everything: friends, comfort, safety and the security of His family home to give us an abundant life. Why? So we would enjoy the riches that knowing Him intimately affords.

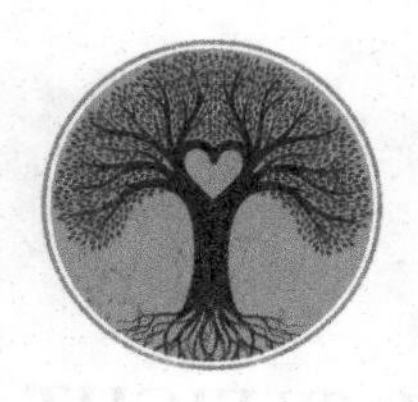

# WEEK THIRTY EIGHT

WEDNESDAY

*Selflessness*

*Even if I am to be poured out as a drink offering upon*
*the sacrificial offering of your faith,*
*I am glad and rejoice with you all.*

Philippians 2:17

---

Paul was a religious leader before he surrendered his life to Christ. He was born into an affluent family, was well educated and lived by the letter of the Mosaic Law. He was a zealot and also a legalist. But after meeting Jesus on the road to Damascus his whole life changed. He started preaching the gospel message, planting churches, helping people learn the truth about Jesus Christ, life and eternity. All the formal education he had acquired…the prestige and power he'd obsessed over for so long…he declares in scripture that it became like rubbish compared to knowing and serving Jesus. Amen.

# WEEK THIRTY EIGHT

THURSDAY *Selflessness*

*For God so loved the world, that he gave his only Son,*
*that whoever believes in him*
*should not perish but have eternal life.*

John 3:16

God the Father sent His Son to die for *our* sin in order to save *us* from hell and bless us with the gift of eternal life. Jesus did what His Father wanted Him to do voluntarily and without bitterness in His heart. No one forced Him to climb up on the cross and do what He did. When He left heaven and came to earth He knew exactly what He was getting into and He came anyway. He loved us that much. He came because He wanted the best for us. So He died in our place canceling the debt we owed…reconciling us to the Father by faith. That's what selflessness looks like. Jesus is our perfect example of how we are to live.

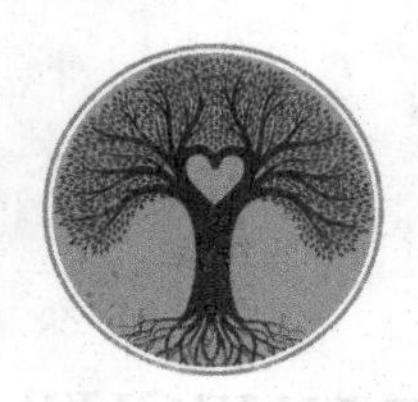

# WEEK THIRTY EIGHT

FRIDAY

*Selflessness*

*In all things I have shown you*
*that by working hard in this way*
*we must help the weak and remember the words of the Lord Jesus,*
*how he himself said,*
*'It is more blessed to give than to receive.'*

Acts 20:35

---

Our culture is held captive by the erroneous notion that life is about us. We strive after the highest form of education…the most prestigious and highest paying jobs so we can earn the big bucks and buy lots of stuff we don't need and can't afford. History proves that we've got it all wrong. According to God life is about knowing Him and serving others. It's pretty obvious that our thinking has been twisted and must be reformed.

God created life. He knows what it's for. We can argue with Him all we want, and do, but it won't get us anywhere. In God's economy, which is the only one that matters, life is about knowing, loving and enjoying Him. Think about it! It just may save your life.

# WEEK THIRTY EIGHT

SATURDAY/SUNDAY *Selflessness*

## Facts of Life:

-Jesus gave His life away.

-We all have something of value to contribute.

-There's always something you can do.

Personal Reflections:

# WEEK THIRTY NINE

MONDAY

*Honesty*

*He who has clean hands and a pure heart,*
*who does not lift up his soul to what is false*
*and does not swear deceitfully.*
*He will receive blessing from the LORD*
*and righteousness from the God of his salvation.*

Psalm 24:4-5

Honesty is important to God. His standards are high. He tells us the truth and expects us to do the same. God never lies and we are His children. We should aspire to follow His perfect example and be just like Him.

Not only does God tell us the truth about everything and what He requires of us but He also explains how He treats us with favor when we strive to be holy as He is holy and live a pure life. Obviously we don't obey God to get anything from Him. We obey God because we love Him and He deserves our obedience.

# WEEK THIRTY NINE

TUESDAY *Honesty*

*Lying lips are an abomination to the LORD,*
*but those who act faithfully are his delight.*

Proverbs 12:22

---

God detests lying. On the other hand He delights in those who speak the truth. That is a humbling fact of life that we should take to heart. On the one hand we make God angry when we lie; on the other hand when we speak truth, words of thanksgiving and encouragement...that brings Him great pleasure and joy.

Our heavenly Father is always with us, watching over us and aware of every thought we think and every word we say. He isn't engaged in our lives to censor and catch us in bad behavior so He can punish us. He just loves us bunches and we matter to Him.

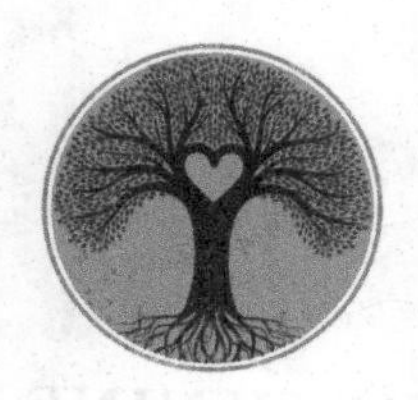

# WEEK THIRTY NINE

WEDNESDAY

*Honesty*

*He will dwell on the heights;*
*his place of defense will be the fortresses of rocks;*
*his bread will be given him; his water will be sure.*

Isaiah 33:16

God created us in His image. He is holy. Life is all about learning more about His nature and character and, via His sweet grace, being more like Him.

It stands to reason then, that since we were made in His image, we will be happier and spiritually healthier when we personally know the truth about God and imitate Him. He promised that He will complete the work He started in us no matter how long it takes. He calls us to lives of honesty and holiness. We can do both if we surrender and allow ourselves to be transformed by His divine power working in us. What a strange and wonderful thing.

# WEEK THIRTY NINE

THURSDAY *Honesty*

*Do not bear false witness.*

Mark 10:19

---

*Bearing false witness.* It may sound like an archaic notion to our polluted and sophisticated minds but the Bible says that *all* scripture is God-breathed and eternal. That means this command in Mark 10 is as applicable and potentially life changing today as it was the day it was written.

We may live *in* this modern world but, as children of God, we are called to be different than everyone else. We don't have to jump on the band wagon and be mean spirited, tell tales and gossip. We're not supposed to. We belong to God and have been set apart for His use, purpose and glory. Speaking words of truth, light and hope into this dark world – *That's our job and joy!*

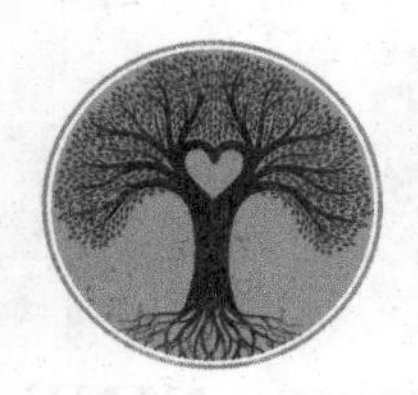

# WEEK THIRTY NINE

FRIDAY

*Honesty*

*Do to others as you would have them do to you.*

Luke 6:31 (KJV)

---

It's so simple. We tend to make everything so complicated. Treating others the way we want to be treated will change the world and make it a better, more peaceful and joy-filled place.

"Self"-centeredness gets us into trouble. We're so busy thinking about ourselves we forget to care about others. In a very real sense we are held captive by what we think, want and feel we deserve. In the end we forfeit the privilege of caring more about others than we do ourselves and pleasing Jesus. Jesus was self-*less*. We can be too.

# WEEK THIRTY NINE

SATURDAY/SUNDAY

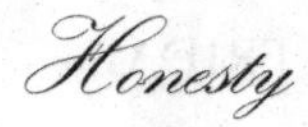

Facts of Life:

-Honesty is important to God.

-God knows our every thought and
hears every word we speak.

-Treat others the way you want to be treated.

Personal Reflections:

# WEEK FORTY

MONDAY

## *Talking with God*

*Pray without ceasing.*

I Thessalonians 5:17

Prayer is an attitude of the heart, really, a longing that leads us into the very presence of God where we can enjoy a private and sweet conversation with Him. It's not just about talking *to* God. It's also about learning how to listen for God…recognizing and responding to His voice. All He wants to do is love us and lead us into the best possible life. Yes, of course, He's interested in what we have to say, but He also wants to tell us the truth about Himself and reveal the plan He has for our lives. Ultimately, He longs for us to draw close so He can give Himself to us in incredible ways. The undeserved and supernatural connection we have with God is, in fact, the very essence of life.

## WEEK FORTY

TUESDAY *Talking with God*

*If my people who are called by my name humble themselves,*
*and pray and seek my face and turn from their wicked ways,*
*then I will hear from heaven and will forgive their sin*
*and heal their land.*

II Chronicles 7:14

God blesses the humble and pours out His favor onto those who turn from sin and pray. God intended to be involved and actively participate in each of our lives. It brings Him great pleasure when we give Him full access to our hearts. When we humble ourselves, seek His face and pray He draws near to us, provides for our every need and shares with us His eternal wisdom and power.

In a way prayer is a matter of acknowledging that God *is* God and that we need Him. The course of human history proves that we all do. Our lives are transformed when we humble ourselves and surrender to His plan and will.

## WEEK FORTY

WEDNESDAY *Talking with God*

*The Lord has heard my plea;*
*the Lord accepts my prayer.*

Psalm 6:9

This is one of the all-time greatest facts of life: *God hears our prayers.* We talk to God, and He listens. *It's beyond incredible!* He listens to what we have to say and cares about what we feel because we are important to Him. He's not interested in taking away our freedom and ruining our lives. He listens because He loves us and wants the best for us. As unfathomable as it may sound we are valuable to Him.

God speaks to those who take the time to listen. Our lives would be be oh so different and sweeter and better if we learned how to listen.

## WEEK FORTY

THURSDAY *Talking with God*

*Now Jesus was praying in a certain place,*
*and when he finished, one of his disciples said to him,*
*"Lord, teach us to pray, as John taught his disciples."*

Luke 11:1

Prayer is a phenomenon. Even the disciples wanted Jesus to teach them how to pray. Opening up our lives and hearts to God can be a bit intimating at first; but at the same time it can be the sweetest, most powerful and enjoyable aspect of life.

Prayer links heaven and earth, God's supernatural Spirit with our flesh and is the life's blood of our relationship with Jesus. It is the single most powerful resource that will insure we succeed in life. In God's presence we are loved and filled with His grace. There is a whole lot to gain when we pray and a great to lose when we don't.

# WEEK FORTY

FRIDAY

*Talking with God*

*And after he had dismissed the crowds,*
*he went up on the mountain by himself to pray.*

Matthew 14:23

---

Jesus was busier and more in demand in His short life than we will ever be. He was surrounded by needy people continuously... teaching, preaching, serving, healing, loving...always giving everything He had to give. Still He disengaged from the crowds and ministerial duties to spend time with His Father.

The healthy margins Jesus established around His life are significant. They provided Jesus with an opportunity to not only physically and emotionally rest but, also, refocus His attention on His Father. If Jesus needed to pray, obviously so do we.

## WEEK FORTY

SATURDAY/SUNDAY *Talking with God*

Facts of Life:

-A never ending conversation with Jesus should be the norm.

-God still speaks to those who take the time to listen.

-Prayer is the single most powerful form of communication.

Personal Reflections:

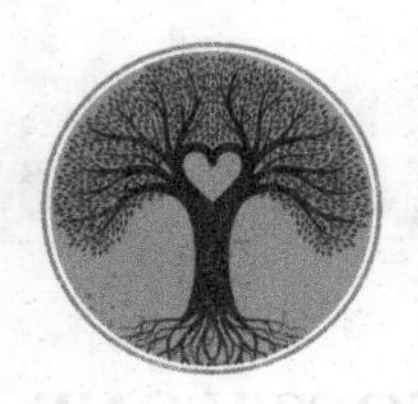

# WEEK FORTY ONE

MONDAY

## *Being Real*

*I praise you, for I am fearfully and wonderfully made.*
*Wonderful are your works;*
*my soul knows it very well.*
*My frame was not hidden from you,*
*when I was being made in secret,*
*intricately woven in the depths of the earth.*

Psalm 139:14-15

---

God made you. And He made you the way you are for a reason. You are not perfect any more than anybody else. Far from it! There will always be lessons for us to learn and room for personal growth. But by God's ingenious design we *are* in the process of becoming incredible works of art.

And when God formed us in our mother's womb He equipped us with talents, strengths and abilities that are uniquely our own. He gave them to us so we would be able to accomplish a certain job down here on earth.

So we spend time with God so we can find out who He created us to be and what He designed us to do. Then, ultimately, we find life's greatest joy being true to our God-given identity.

# WEEK FORTY ONE

TUESDAY

*Being Real*

*Before I formed you in the womb I knew you,*
*and before you were born I consecrated you;*
*I appointed you a prophet to the nations.*

Jeremiah 1:5

---

It's hard to wrap our minds around, but God *"knew"* us before time began. "Knew" in the sense that He recognized *who* and *what* He would create us to be. Then, as He personally got involved in forming us, He handpicked certain strengths, talents and abilities that we would need to do the good work He ordained us to do. The miracle is – we have everything we need to fulfill God's plan and purpose for our lives. That's why trying to be someone we're not doesn't work. Being inauthentic is exhausting and a big fat waste of time.

# WEEK FORTY ONE

WEDNESDAY

*Being Real*

*For I know the plans I have for you, declares the LORD,*
*plans for welfare and not for evil, to give you a future and a hope.*

Jeremiah 29:11

---

God wants to bless us. That's why He created us. We didn't evolve from some primordial puddle of goo. The Lord God Almighty made us with the intention of giving us a future and a hope and a job to perform.

We won't all be great theologians, brain surgeons and athletic superstars. That's because we're all different by God's design. You are designed by God to be a certain someone and to do some important and specific something. The same is true for me. Success in life and personal satisfaction is experienced by those who surrender their lives to God and carry out His will. And of course He is pleased and glorified when we do.

# WEEK FORTY ONE

THURSDAY *Being Real*

*See to it that no one takes you captive by*
*philosophy and empty deceit,*
*according to human tradition, according to*
*the elemental spirits of the world,*
*and not according to Christ. For in him the*
*whole fullness of deity dwells bodily,*
*and you have been filled in him, who is the*
*head of all rule and authority.*

Colossians 2:8-10

---

God is enough. We are "complete" to overflowing *in* Him. There will always be people who will tell us that we can't do something…that whatever we're thinking about getting involved in is impossible and we shouldn't waste our time. But if God moves us in a certain direction…if His Spirit prompts us to do a particular something, even if at first it seems beyond our reach, all we have to do is step out in faith and the Lord will show up in all His glory and do whatever needs to be done. We are not called to a life of self-sufficiency but told to walk by faith.

Fixating on personal opinion…what other people think…won't get us where God wants us to go. Believing and trusting in Jesus will.

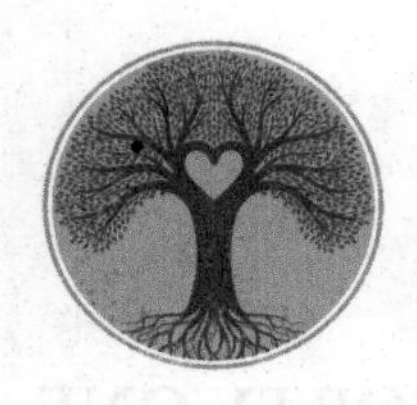

# WEEK FORTY ONE

FRIDAY

*Being Real*

*And he gave the apostles, the prophets, the evangelists,*
*the shepherds and teachers, to equip the*
*saints for the work of ministry,*
*for building up the body of Christ,*
*until we all attain to the unity of the faith and*
*of the knowledge of the Son of God,*
*to mature manhood, to the measure of the*
*stature of the fullness of Christ.*

Ephesians 4:11-13

We are all "gifted" and have something of great value to offer. God made sure of that. God gave each and every one of us at least one spiritual gift that comes alive at the moment of our redemption and spiritual rebirth. These "gifts" equip us to do the work He created and assigned for us to do, whether it is building up His church, loving the unlovable or evangelizing the world. The key is to use what we've been given for God's purposes and glory.

## WEEK FORTY ONE

SATURDAY/SUNDAY

*Being Real*

| Facts of Life: |
|---|
| -God made us. |
| -God has a plan for our lives. |
| -We are members of God's royal family. |

Personal Reflections:

# WEEK FORTY TWO

MONDAY

*Sympathy*

*Two are better than one, because they have*
*a good reward for their toil.*
*For if they fall, one will lift up his fellow.*
*But woe to him who is alone when he falls*
*and has not another to lift him up!*

Ecclesiastes 4:9-10

---

We are *not* islands unto ourselves, whether we want to be or not. That is one reason why our heavenly Father emphasizes the importance of loving one another in His Word. Love is a priority with Him.

I don't know when it got started, maybe when Adam and Eve did their thing in the Garden, but for some reason humans have adopted an adversarial attitude when it comes to personal relationships. Maybe it has something to do with our self-centeredness and wills. We tend to ignore the fact that, regardless of race, color or creed, we're all members of the human race. Instead of helping one another we compete, argue and fight with each other. That's not what God wants or intended. He wants us to have compassion and sympathize with one another. Of course it's not easy, but we can.

# WEEK FORTY TWO

TUESDAY

*Sympathy*

*Bear one another's burdens, and so fulfill the law of Christ.*

Galatians 6:2

---

Where would we be if Jesus hadn't climbed up on that cross and died for our sin? What would have happened if He hadn't sympathized with our weakness and had compassion for our lost souls? In His Word the Lord tells us to rejoice with those who rejoice and weep with those who weep. We need to genuinely listen to each other and be interested in what's going on in each other's lives.

Being attentive and listening is one of the most powerful and effective ways to show we truly care. It demonstrates to people that they are loved and they are not alone.

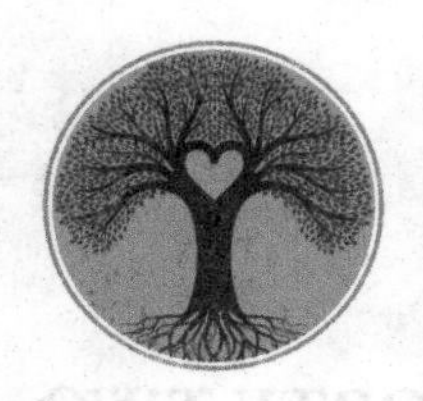

# WEEK FORTY TWO

WEDNESDAY *Sympathy*

*On the day I called, you answered me;*
*my strength of soul you increased.*

Psalm 138:3

King David cried out to God and prayed. Apparently the way God answered David's prayer surpassed David's expectations. God's like that. He delights in surprising us with His love and supernatural power.

One thing that absolutely amazes me about God is the way He sympathizes with our weakness and, in general, the human condition. But He does it all the time and in a multiplicity of unexpected ways. God is perfectly aware of not only our short comings and feels bad when we find ourselves in a challenging situation but He expects us to do the same for one another. Imagine what life would be like if we learned to love the way He loves?

# WEEK FORTY TWO

THURSDAY

*Sympathy*

*Therefore, confess your sins to one another and pray for one another, that you may be healed.*
*The prayer of a righteous person has great power as it is working.*

James 5:16

---

Here's the key to caring. It's not just the confessing our personal sin to one another bit, but the praying *for* one another part of this verse that makes the difference. Praying for and with one another is what is ultimately important and changes things. Prayer isn't a luxury. It's an absolute necessity when it comes to success and true prosperity in the Christian life. It's during those sacred moments of prayer…in God's presence…when the power of heaven is brought down from heaven to earth. Besides…it pleases God and makes Him smile.

# WEEK FORTY TWO

FRIDAY *Sympathy*

*Now may our Lord Jesus Christ himself, and God our Father,*
*who loved us and gave us eternal comfort*
*and good hope through grace,*
*comfort your hearts and establish them*
*in every good work and word.*

II Thessalonians 2:16-17

God knows us inside out and loves us anyway. His wants to walk alongside us through life and provide us with everything we need to personally excel, spiritually succeed and prosper. He longs for our success even more than we do and will fill us with the fullness of His grace if we let Him. And that's when we can share with others what we received from Him.

Everyone is a vital and valuable member of the human race. We are all related and members of one big created and loved-by-God family. Therefore, it is our privilege and responsibility to love one another. The world will be a happier and much better place if we do.

## WEEK FORTY TWO

SATURDAY/SUNDAY *Sympathy*

Facts of Life:

-Two are better than one.

-We need each other.

-Divine things happen when we do life together and share.

Personal Reflections:

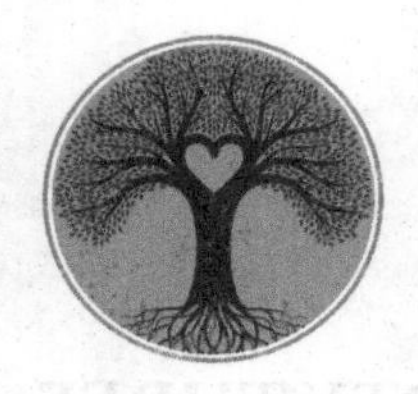

# WEEK FORTY THREE

MONDAY

## *The Ultimate Workout*

*Therefore, my beloved, as you have always obeyed, so now,*
*not only as in my presence but much more in my absence,*
*work out your own salvation with fear and trembling,*
*for it is God who works in you,*
*both to will and to work for his good pleasure.*

Philippians 2:12-13

---

Jesus saves us from hell. He does His part, which is obviously something only He can do. But even after our initial salvation experience there is work that must be done, and it's ours to do. The Bible says that after placing our faith in Jesus we are to spend our lives seeking and growing in our personal knowledge of Him. That's the part we're supposed to play and the way we can succeed while we walk down here on planet earth.

All of this would be impossible if Jesus hadn't sent His Spirit to live in us. But He did. So you see…what God tells us to do…we *can* do. There's hope for us yet!

## WEEK FORTY THREE

TUESDAY *The Ultimate Workout*

*But I say, walk by the Spirit, and you will*
*not gratify the desires of the flesh.*
*For the desires of the flesh are against the Spirit, and the desires*
*of the Spirit are against the flesh, for these are opposed to each*
*other, to keep you from doing the things you want to do.*

Galatians 5:16-17

---

We're all rebels at heart. We inherited Adam's predisposition to rebel, how could we not be? And that rebel's heart is how we get ourselves into so much trouble. It's the best we can do apart from Jesus. Totally surrendering our lives to Him is our only hope. But when we give up the control of our lives Jesus steps in and makes something special of our lives. He reforms our thinking…pours His graces into our souls and accomplishes the impossible when we corporate with Him. He is committed and has promised to do His part. The question is…will we do ours?

# WEEK FORTY THREE

WEDNESDAY *The Ultimate Workout*

*But the fruit of the Spirit is love, joy, peace, patience, kindness, goodness, faithfulness, gentleness, self-control; against such things there is no law.*

Galatians 5:22-23

---

God has placed all sorts of supernatural resources at our disposal. Who wouldn't long for peace, living in the crazy and chaotic world we do? Is there anyone who doesn't want to love and be loved unconditionally? Can anyone honestly say they *don't* crave joy and contentment? Wouldn't you like to be self-controlled instead of being out of control? Well, God has a plan and wants to bless us today and every day with every one of these things. All we have to do is walk in God's Spirit and accept the plan He has for our lives.

# WEEK FORTY THREE

THURSDAY *The Ultimate Workout*

*And walk in love, as Christ loved us and gave himself up for us, a fragrant offering and sacrifice to God.*

Ephesians 5:2

---

Our life in Christ is all about laying aside our self-centeredness and opening ourselves up to the will and transforming love of God. His divine and supernatural power is already at work in us. When we receive His love and put ourselves under His sovereign authority...our natural propensity towards self-centeredness is replaced with His divine love and *selflessness.*

No! We can't possibly love the way Jesus loves on our own. But we *can* with His help.

# WEEK FORTY THREE

FRIDAY

## *The Ultimate Workout*

*For sin will have no dominion over you,*
*since you are not under law but under grace.*

Romans 6:14

---

We became new creations when Jesus saved our souls. From the moment of our conversion He has been working to show us a different, better and God-honoring way to live life. Think of the whole process as the ultimate makeover.

The exciting thing is…learning how to have a walk worthy of Christ isn't about *self*-improvement. If we want to achieve our divine potential and enjoy the life Jesus died to give us we have to learn to do things His way not our own. Oh, and by the way, it *does* take a bit of getting used to.

# WEEK FORTY THREE

SATURDAY/SUNDAY *The Ultimate Workout*

## Facts of Life:

-The goal is to become more like Jesus.

-He has placed His divine power at our disposal.

-God has a perfect plan for your life.

Personal Reflections:

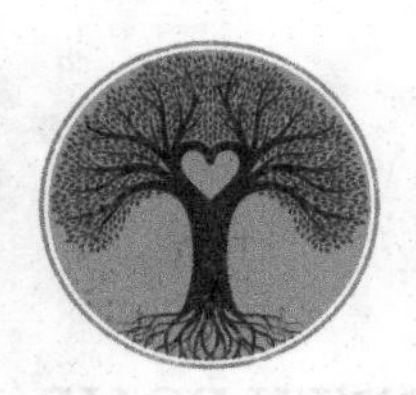

# WEEK FORTY FOUR

MONDAY

*Jesus*

John 1:1-5

---

This passage of scripture may sound a bit confusing at first… until you realize that John is talking about his cousin, Jesus. The "Word," Jesus, was in heaven with His Father and the Holy Spirit and then…*voila*…He created everything, literally.

Jesus created all that was created, including you and me. He died to save us from our sin and gives us the gift of a new and abundant life. Apart from a personal relationship with Jesus there's no hope of abundance, not in ways that truly matter. But *with* Jesus… there is love, light, purpose, peace and divine power. Why would we choose to live apart from Him?

# WEEK FORTY FOUR

TUESDAY *Jesus*

Luke 2:1-7

---

The Creator of Everything and Savior of the World was born in a stable. It was a humble beginning to a miraculous life. Still, Jesus' entrance into this world changed the course of human history.

It's astonishing to think that Jesus chose to enter His earthly existence in such a less than extravagant and self-grandizing way. And yes, He did have a choice in the matter. There was no pomp and circumstance when it came to Jesus' lowly birth…no stretch limos or red carpet to stroll down. He could have had all those things. He was God! Instead, He was born in a stable, served those He loved and died in a humble way. Now that's impressive.

# WEEK FORTY FOUR

WEDNESDAY *Jesus*

*Have this mind among yourselves, which is yours in Christ Jesus,*
*who, though he was in the form of God, did not count equality*
*with God a thing to be grasped, but emptied himself,*
*by taking the form of a servant, being born in the likeness of men.*
*And being found in human form,*
*he humbled himself by becoming obedient to the point of death,*
*even death on a cross.*

Philippians 2:5-8

---

Jesus didn't exploit the fact that He was God or use His position and authority for selfish gain. Instead of exalting Himself, He gave His rights away and became a slave to all. With a type of humility and grace that had never been seen before on earth, or since, Jesus accepted the role He was destined to play without complaint or resentment. His humble birth, rather obscure life and brutal death were all about saving those He created from hell and glorifying His Father in heaven.

Odd the way one inexplicable act of servitude forever changed the world.

## WEEK FORTY FOUR

THURSDAY *Jesus*

*What do you think? If a man has a hundred*
*sheep, and one of them has gone astray,*
*does he not leave the ninety-nine on the mountains*
*and go in search of the one that went astray?*
*And if he finds it, truly, I say to you,*
*he rejoices over it more than over the ninety-*
*nine that never went astray.*
*So it is not the will of my Father*
*who is in heaven that one of these little ones should perish.*

Matthew 18:11-14

---

Everyone matters to God. There are no exceptions. He looks at every person: their past, present and future as a loved, valuable and potential work of art.

One of the greatest encouragements we can experience as human beings is to know that we belong to God and that He truly cherishes us. He is at our side. He always will be. We are never alone. And He is on our side. None of this will ever change. Knowing that we are important and loved by God should change the way we see ourselves, others and live our lives. Really, the fact of God's love should change everything.

# WEEK FORTY FOUR

FRIDAY

*Jesus*

*Therefore, since we are surrounded by so great a cloud of witnesses, let us also lay aside every weight, and sin which clings so closely, and let us run with endurance the race that is set before us, looking to Jesus, the founder and perfecter of our faith, who for the joy that was set before him endured the cross, despising the shame, and is seated at the right hand of the throne of God.*

Hebrews 12:1-3

---

Life can be a bit of a challenge. That's why we need to fix our eyes on Jesus and recount all the good He has already done for us. If we fixate on the negative circumstances we're enduring down here on earth, we're bound to be overwhelmed, anxious and get depressed. That's why it's so important for us to talk with Jesus about what's going on and how we feel…thank Him for everything He's done in the past…recount His many blessings and receive His grace so we can succeed in the present. Spending time with Jesus can cure whatever ails us. Truly, it does!

## WEEK FORTY FOUR

SATURDAY/SUNDAY

| Facts of Life: |
| --- |
| -You are loved, cherished and valued by God. |
| -Fix your eyes on Jesus, especially when life gets hard. |
| -Jesus died so you could live abundantly. |

Personal Reflections:

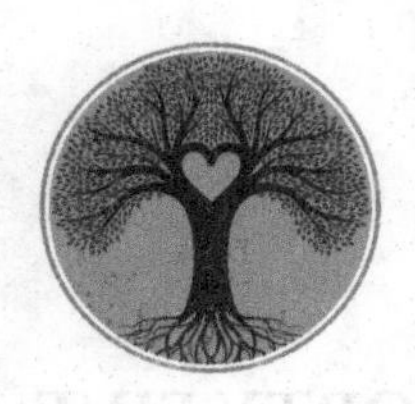

# WEEK FORTY FIVE

MONDAY *Fear*

Deuteronomy 6:1-3

God says, *"Don't be afraid."* Sure there are all sorts of things in this scary world that can make us anxious. But God doesn't want us to walk through life afraid of anyone or anything. Instead, He wants us to trust him. And when we consider how much He loves us all the scary stuff in this world seems to fall away.

Fearing God however is a whole different thing. We're not supposed to be terrified of God. The *"fear"* Moses talks about in Deuteronomy is about standing in awe of God and respecting Him. God invites us to know Him and experience the full extent of His loves. There's no better way to live life?

## WEEK FORTY FIVE

TUESDAY *Fear*

*The LORD is my light and my salvation;*
*whom shall I fear?*
*The LORD is the stronghold of my life;*
*of whom shall I be afraid?*

Psalm 27:1

Who will I fear? Obviously that's a rhetorical question. David, the greatest warrior king of Israel, knew there was nothing in this life to fear. He understood experientially that God was on his side beyond a shadow of a doubt. And...with God in our lives watching over us...with God running interference for us and fighting the enemy on our behalf...what's there to be afraid of?

David wasn't earth bound in his thinking. He knew God loved him and was able to do anything and everything that needed to be done to keep him safe and alive. We can walk in the same kind of absolute faith.

# WEEK FORTY FIVE

WEDNESDAY *Fear*

*The fear of the LORD is the beginning of wisdom;*
*all those who practice it have a good understanding.*
*His praise endures forever!*

Psalm 111:10

---

Earlier in the Book of Psalm David declared that *"there was no fear of God."* The King was stating what was true about the culture he lived in. And here in Psalm 111, David addresses the issue of *fear* and *respect* for God again. Without apology, he explains that learning to *"fear"* God is the first step that leads to living life as God intended it to be lived.

Seeking the Lord and loving Him with our whole being is what we were created for. It is this seeking and loving God that fulfills the human soul and creates an intimate relationship with God and makes life worth living.

## WEEK FORTY FIVE

THURSDAY *Fear*

*Be strong; fear not!*
*Behold, your God*
*will come with vengeance,*
*with the recompense of God.*
*He will come and save you.*

Isaiah 35:4

---

It is God's job to forgive our sin and save us from hell. He can do for us what we cannot possibly do for ourselves. Our job is to love, respect and put our trust in Him.

Living in a fallen world the way we do we're bound to bump up against all sorts of scary stuff that can make us afraid. But we don't have to be afraid. God's doesn't want us to be afraid because He is on our side. He is with us. He is for us and fighting the enemy on our behalf. We can live fear bound lives all our lives if we choose to…or we can put our trust in Him. It is our choice. We get to choose.

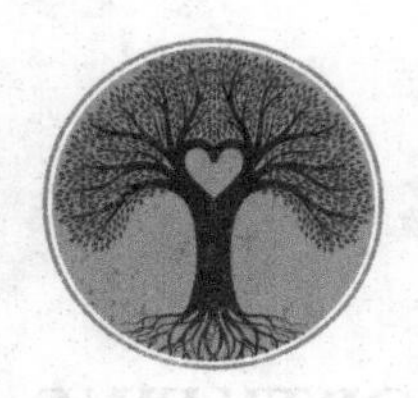

# WEEK FORTY FIVE

FRIDAY *Fear*

*Peace I leave with you; my peace I give to you.*
*Not as the world gives do I give to you.*
*Let not your hearts be troubled,*
*neither let them be afraid.*

John 14:27

Jesus came to earth, died for our sin and sent His Spirit to live in us so we could live an abundant life. He went to a lot of trouble and paid the ultimate price to bless us with the extraordinary gift of life. He tells us to be strong and courageous and doesn't want us to be afraid. Instead we are. He wants us to put our trust in Him. He has a perfect plan for each of our lives which includes a future infused with bunches of supernatural strength, courage as well as heavenly hope. His Spirit lives in us as believer. He is our Constant Companion and wants to be our Bestest Friend. On top of all that...He cares more about our success and prosperity than we do.

## WEEK FORTY FIVE

SATURDAY/SUNDAY

Facts of Life:

-God deserves our reverence and respect.

-There's nothing to be afraid of.

-Seek Jesus first. He's got everything under control,

Personal Reflections:

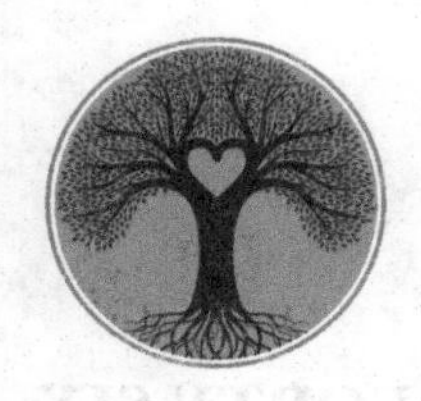

# WEEK FORTY SIX

MONDAY *Holiness*

*Do you not know that you are God's temple*
*and that God's Spirit dwells in you?*

I Corinthians 3:16

---

Jesus set us apart when He saved our souls. We belong to Him. He sent His Spirit to live in us so we can know Him intimately and achieve our divine potential…do the good works He ordained us to do. I know it's hard to wrap our minds around all this good stuff. It is so beyond the realm of human understanding. But let's face it, our relationship with Jesus has little, if anything, to do with human logic and reason. The Lord's ways are not our ways. They're better, way better. The ultimate fact of life is that God tells us the truth about everything. EVERYTHING! That means we can rejoice in His truth whether we understand everything or not.

## WEEK FORTY SIX

TUESDAY *Holiness*

*Therefore, since we are surrounded by so great a cloud of witnesses,*
*let us also lay aside every weight,*
*and sin which clings so closely,*
*and let us run with endurance the race that is set before us.*

Hebrews 12:1

Fixing our eyes on Jesus is an absolute necessity if we want to live a peaceful and holy life. Holiness isn't about *self*-improvement. It's about walking by faith and obedience.

It is liberating to recognize that our "holiness" is accomplished by God's sweet grace and not human effort. Like our initial salvation…aspiring to be more like Jesus is all about letting Him do *for* us, *in* and *through* us what we cannot possibly do for ourselves. Remember, Jesus is perfect and He can do anything.

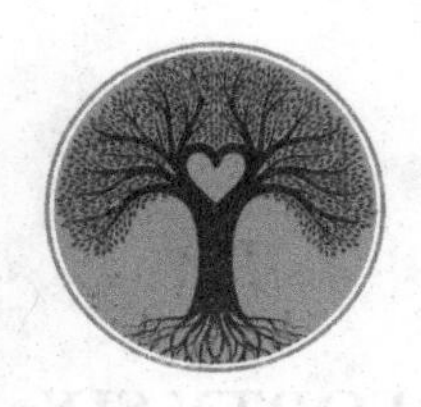

## WEEK FORTY SIX

WEDNESDAY *Holiness*

*For this very reason, make every effort to*
*supplement your faith with virtue,*
*and virtue with knowledge, and knowledge with self-control,*
*and self-control with steadfastness, and steadfastness with godliness,*
*and godliness with brotherly affection, and*
*brotherly affection with love.*
*For if these qualities are yours and are increasing,*
*they keep you from being ineffective*
*or unfruitful in the knowledge of our Lord Jesus Christ.*

II Peter 1:5-8

Jesus gives us life and saves our souls. He sends His Spirit to live in us so we can know Him and become the people He intended us to be.

Before Jesus there was no way we could ever reach our full potential or succeed at life, not really. Now we can. And yes, even after Jesus enters into our lives we will still face some challenges and trials. We're bound to. But in Jesus' divine economy those challenges and trails will serve a purpose. They will humble our souls and force us to turn to and depend on Him. Just think – Every moment of every day God the Father is working to conform us to the image of His Son.

## WEEK FORTY SIX

THURSDAY *Holiness*

*I appeal to you therefore, brothers, by the mercies of God,*
*to present your bodies as a living sacrifice,*
*holy and acceptable to God, which is your spiritual worship.*

Romans 12:1

Old Testament worshippers used to enter into a temple and offer sacrifices to Jehovah as, both, an act of obedience and worship. It was a way they could demonstrate their love for God by submitting to Him. When Jesus came He put a new system into place. Now, as an act of worship and way of demonstrating our love for God, we get to present our *"bodies,"* our lives to God and aspire to live pure and holy lives before Him.

We give everything we are and everything we have to God because we love Him, not out of a bitter sense of obligation.

# WEEK FORTY SIX

FRIDAY *Holiness*

*Turn away from evil and do good;*
*so shall you dwell forever.*

Psalm 37:27

*Depart from evil and do good.* Sounds simple, right? It's the doing of the thing with a glad heart that can be hard. The mystery of living the Christian life is that God never tells us to do anything we cannot do with His help. His grace is sufficient and divine strength is enough.

Yes. We are to study God's Word, but it's not about accumulating a bunch of head knowledge. The Bible says that we are to be *doers* of God's Word. Our holiness is possible because of Jesus. And someday...when we get to heaven and stand face to face with Him, we will be like Him. *Can you imagine?*

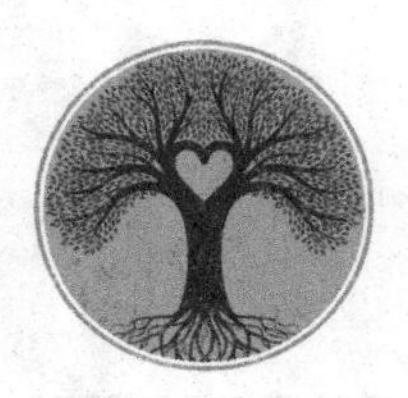

## WEEK FORTY SIX

SATURDAY/SUNDAY

Facts of Life:

-Holiness isn't about self-improvement. It's about fixing our eyes on Jesus and being more like Him.

-Surrender and obedience leads to holiness.

-We are God's representatives on earth.

Personal Reflections:

# WEEK FORTY SEVEN

MONDAY *Purity*

*Have mercy on me, O God,*
*according to your steadfast love;*
*according to your abundant mercy*
*blot out my transgressions.*

Psalm 51:1

*"Create in me a clean heart, O God."* That needs to be the cry of everyone's heart. We're human and, unfortunately, bad stuff has a peculiar and tenacious way of finding its way into our souls. We get confused, discouraged and develop a poor attitude as a result. The way of finding our way out of the muddle is to turn to God and ask for His help…ask Him to let us see our circumstances and what's happening in our lives through His eyes.

Confessing to God that we're having a hard time and need help is a good thing. It humbles our spirits and puts us in a position whereby we can receive His best.

## WEEK FORTY SEVEN

TUESDAY *Purity*

*Come now, let us reason together, says the* L*ORD:*
*though your sins are like scarlet,*
*they shall be as white as snow;*
*though they are red like crimson,*
*they shall become like wool.*

Isaiah 1:18

God is the only one who can forgive sin. He alone has the divine power required to cleanse us from sin and help us do what is right and keep us from doing wrong. Jesus sacrificed His life to give us a chance to live an abundant life and sent His Spirit to live in us so we would be able to walk humbly and purely with our God.

Walking in the Spirit and following Jesus is the way to experience and enjoy a truly abundant life. That's the bottom line.

# WEEK FORTY SEVEN

WEDNESDAY *Purity*

*Blessed are the pure in heart, for they shall see God.*

Matthew 5:8

The Bible says that the human heart is deceptive and desperately wicked. We are weak, finite beings and everything we see, hear and experience can leave a negative imprint on our souls.

Everyone is responsible to live a pure and righteous life before God. We belong to Him. We are members of His royal family and, therefore, ambassadors for Christ. Purity is about keeping our minds, bodies and souls unpolluted by the things of this world. And we *can* do that. The Bible says that "*We can do all things through Christ who strengthens us* (Philippians 4:13)."

# WEEK FORTY SEVEN

THURSDAY *Purity*

*Finally, brothers, whatever is true, whatever is honorable,*
*whatever is just, whatever is pure, whatever*
*is lovely, whatever is commendable,*
*if there is any excellence, if there is anything*
*worthy of praise, think about these things.*

Philippians 4:8

What we expose our minds to matters. Our thoughts have an enormous influence on our lives and can change, for good or bad, how we behave. If our thoughts are in a constant state of turmoil, negativity and worry eventually they will have an unhealthy impact on our souls and lives. Our perspective and attitude will be dramatically altered when we take Paul's advice. When we trust Jesus instead of being anxious we become the positive, joy-filled and optimistic people God intended us to be. Then we can share with others what we received from Him.

# WEEK FORTY SEVEN

FRIDAY *Purity*

*If we confess our sins, he is faithful*
*and just to forgive us our sins*
*and to cleanse us from all unrighteousness.*

I John 1:9

When we sin the best thing to do is talk to God about it. He knows what we've done anyway. He knows everything. And when we humble ourselves and agree with Him that what we've done is wrong and ask for forgiveness...He forgives us. He cleanses our souls. He picks us up, dusts us off and gives us the courage to press on in our attempt to live a pure life before Him.

What we do with our lives affects God. He loves us and we matter to Him. We can't afford to let anything get in the way of our relationship with Him.

## WEEK FORTY SEVEN

SATURDAY/SUNDAY

Facts of Life:

-God cleanses us from sin.

-Confession is good for the soul.

-We can do what God tells us to do.

Personal Reflections:

# WEEK FORTY EIGHT

MONDAY

*Praise*

*I call upon the Lord, who is worthy to be praised,*
*and I am saved from my enemies.*

II Samuel 22:4

---

In this psalm David extols God as his *defense, refuge,* and *deliverer.* David was a lowly shepherd boy that God anointed as a warrior king. He went from leading and protecting his father's sheep – sleeping under the stars, killing lions with his bare hands and giants with a slingshot...to ruling the greatest nation in the world. But when his life circumstances changed he ended up running from his own son in fear for his life.

Yes, David was a man after God's own heart, but he was also human. His life was full of responsibilities, stress and all sorts of problems. Still, David kept his eyes on the Lord and trusted Him.

# WEEK FORTY EIGHT

TUESDAY *Praise*

*I will bless the* L*ORD* *at all times;*
*his praise shall continually be in my mouth.*

Psalm 34:1

---

I will praise God in the dark and when it is light...in the good times and when things are really bad. I will praise God when I have enough and when I'm forced to go without...when I'm healthy and even when I am sick. I'll praise God when my relationships with others are going well...and when they're not.

No matter what is going on in our lives we can and should speak well of God. He is with us all the time...in the midst of everything...trying to work all things together for our ultimate good. *Praise Him.*

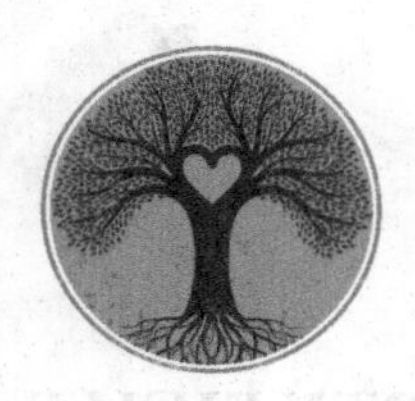

# WEEK FORTY EIGHT

WEDNESDAY *Praise*

*Blessed be the Lord!*
*For he has heard the voice of my pleas for mercy.*
*The Lord is my strength and my shield;*
*in him my heart trusts, and I am helped;*
*my heart exults,*
*and with my song I give thanks to him.*

Psalm 28:6-7

We all have needs and God is willing to provide for those needs. The reality is we can't do without Him and He *can* be trusted. He is faithful. People may want to help us, but sometimes they can't. God is different. He's GOD! And He never fails or disappoints. He bears our burdens and has compassion and even sympathizes with our weakness. He sees our needs and will take good care of us if we humble ourselves and let Him.

Could there possibly be a more steadfast lover and faithful Friend than Him?

# WEEK FORTY EIGHT

THURSDAY *Praise*

Psalm 100:1-5

Is there anything in life more important than knowing God? No! There's not. Knowing God is why He created us in the first place. Knowing Him personally and intimately is the purpose of life as far as He is concerned.

It's odd the way we *expect* God to bless us as if we were entitled. Unfortunately, it goes along with our fallen human condition. According to the psalmist there has to be a paradigm shift in our thinking and challenges us to focus on God instead of ourselves. What a revolutionary concept, right? I wonder what life would be like if we did?

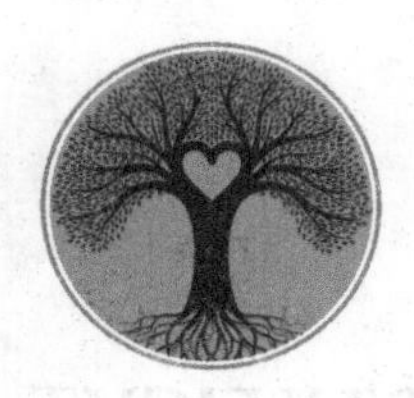

# WEEK FORTY EIGHT

FRIDAY

*Praise*

*Now to him who is able to do far more abundantly*
*than all that we ask or think, according*
*to the power at work within us,*
*to him be glory in the church*
*and in Christ Jesus throughout all generations,*
*forever and ever. Amen.*

Ephesians 3:20-21

---

As human beings we can't even begin to imagine what God wants to do *for* us, *in* us and *through* us. Our minds are too finite to contain all the good He has planned for those who love Him. Think of how long you've been trying to overcome a bad habit, think purer thoughts, love others the way Jesus loves you. Then think about what might happen if you surrendered your life to God and did what He told you to do.

The power of heaven is at your disposal, right now, today, and it always will be. With the Lord on your side you can do anything.

## WEEK FORTY EIGHT

SATURDAY/SUNDAY

Facts of Life:

-Praise God all the time.

-God is the source of true blessing.

-Speak well of God. He deserves it.

Personal Reflections:

# WEEK FORTY NINE

MONDAY *Hope*

*Be strong, and let your heart take courage,*
*all you who wait for the* LORD!*

Psalm 31:24

---

We can do whatever God asks us to do. We are not trapped forever in our human weakness. God is sovereign, faithful and powerful. He can do anything. We may be filled with fear and anxiety, but He is courageous and afraid of nothing. We don't know it all, but He does. And miracle of miracles…God is willing to share all that He is and all that He has with us. He is our hope. With Him on our side there is no limit to what we can do for His glory and the good of His kingdom.

## WEEK FORTY NINE

TUESDAY *Hope*

*Why are you cast down, O my soul,*
*and why are you in turmoil within me?*
*Hope in God; for I shall again praise him,*
*my salvation and my God.*

Psalm 43:5

Everyone gets discouraged from time to time. It's a part of the human condition. Life isn't always fair and people don't always treat us the way we want or think they should.

The good news is – Jesus has a solution to the problem. He loves us and wants the best for us and knows everything. When we don't understand why we're feeling the way we feel…He does. What's more…He can and will lead us out of darkness into His light if we follow Him. Draw near to God and He promised that He would draw near to you.

# WEEK FORTY NINE

WEDNESDAY *Hope*

*Blessed is the man who trusts in the* L*ORD*,
*whose trust is the* L*ORD*.

Jeremiah 17:7

---

When we place our trust in Jesus we find hope. And really, trust is a choice. There are lots of things we don't understand about life and can't do anything about. But what we *can't* do…Jesus can and will do. Let's face it, at best we are feeble and finite human beings...limited in so many ways. But Jesus isn't! There are no limits when it comes to His knowledge, wisdom, love and power. And here is the over the top and amazing part…He's ready and willing to share everything He knows and possesses with you and me.

What else could we possibly need or want?

# WEEK FORTY NINE

THURSDAY *Hope*

*The LORD roars from Zion,*
*and utters his voice from Jerusalem,*
*and the heavens and the earth quake.*
*But the LORD is a refuge to his people,*
*a stronghold to the people of Israel.*

Joel 13:16

---

God has everything under control. It may not always feel like it, but He does. He's on His throne, exercising His sovereign power, even when bad stuff happens and life seems to be falling apart. That means there is hope. The question we have to ask ourselves is "What am I putting my trust in?" Myself? Other people? Fate? World systems? Or am I aligning myself with the will of God and putting my absolute faith in Him? On top of all that...God knows what we truly need better than we do. He wastes nothing and promises to work all things together for our good if we walk by faith and follow Him.

# WEEK FORTY NINE

FRIDAY

*Hope*

*Now may our Lord Jesus Christ himself, and God our Father,*
*who loved us and gave us eternal comfort*
*and good hope through grace,*
*comfort your hearts and establish them*
*in every good work and word.*

II Thessalonian 2:16

God's favor and divine influence is at work in our lives. He is a loving Father and wants to bless those who love Him. The Almighty God of the Universe cares about us. And therein lays our one great hope.

Maybe that's why so many of us stumble through life without hope. We get so entangled in earthly life...running from here to there at breakneck speed...over extending ourselves...getting too involved...that we don't spend time with Jesus and luxuriate in the benefits that being with Him affords. If we did we'd find out that in His infinite and unconditional love there is always hope and no room for despair.

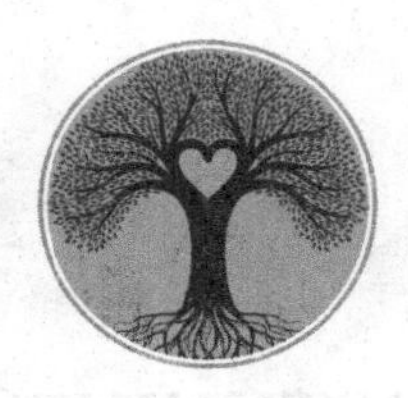

## WEEK FORTY NINE

SATURDAY/SUNDAY

| Facts of Life: |
| --- |
| -God is our one true hope. |
| -Hope is all about trust. |
| -Jesus possesses all things and will share all He has with us. |

Personal Reflections:

# WEEK FIFTY

MONDAY *Learn and Grow*

*Do your best to present yourself to God as one approved,*
*a worker who has no need to be ashamed,*
*rightly handling the word of truth.*

II Timothy 2:15

Christianity is not static. It's not just about receiving the free gift of salvation and then going on with life as usual. No! Being fully engaged and investing ourselves in a faith-based relationship with Jesus Christ is, really, about perpetually seeking God, learning and growing for His glory. Amen.

II Timothy 2:25 tells us to study to show ourselves approved. We study the Bible to learn about God and how to live life the way He wants us to and how to love each other and serve. If we don't read our Bible's how are we supposed to learn?

# WEEK FIFTY

TUESDAY *Learn and Grow*

*If then you have been raised with Christ,*
*seek the things that are above,*
*where Christ is, seated at the right hand of God.*
*Set your minds on things that are above,*
*not on things that are on earth.*
*For you have died, and your life is hidden with Christ in God.*
*When Christ who is your life appears, then you*
*also will appear with him in glory.*

Colossians 3:1-4

Before we gave our lives to Jesus we focused on ourselves and what was happening down here on earth. Now, after conversion, we have more important things to think about and do. That's why the apostle Paul tells us to *"set our minds on things above."* We are "new creations" in Christ. Life is about heavenly matters and learning all we can about Jesus and joining Him in the work He's doing in the world. We study. We pray. We give thanks and worship. We live to please Him. Truly, there isn't a better, richer or more satisfying way to live life.

# WEEK FIFTY

WEDNESDAY *Learn and Grow*

*Therefore, since we are surrounded by so great a cloud of witnesses,*
*let us also lay aside every weight, and sin which clings so closely,*
*and let us run with endurance the race that is set before us,*
*looking to Jesus, the founder and perfecter of our faith,*
*who for the joy that was set before him endured the cross,*
*despising the shame, and is seated at the*
*right hand of the throne of God.*

Hebrews 12:1-2

In an age when physical fitness is lauded as the most important thing, we tend to focus on it the most. But what the author of Hebrews is referring to in today's passage is spiritual fitness. Our Father in Heaven wants us to make sure that we take good care of our souls.

One of the ways we can do that is to keep short accounts with God and daily deal with personal sin. Sin, in any form, big or small, gets in the way of our developing and maintaining an intimate relationship with Jesus. And when we do sin, and we will, we confess it to God and He will forgive us. It's all about maintaining our spiritual health.

# WEEK FIFTY

THURSDAY *Learn and Grow*

*Therefore, my beloved, as you have always obeyed, so now,*
*not only as in my presence but much more in my absence,*
*work out your own salvation with fear and trembling,*
*for it is God who works in you,*
*both to will and to work for his good pleasure.*

Philippians 2:12-13

---

Being a Christian requires some work. Jesus saves us. Obviously that's something we cannot do for ourselves. But when it comes to living for Him…we read His Word, we pray and serve and learn how to love others as He loves us. But most importantly, we spend time in His presence and, by His grace, learn to be humble and selfless as He is humble and selfless. Striving to please the One who breathed life into our lungs and saves us – That is what life is for?

## WEEK FIFTY

FRIDAY

*Learn and Grow*

*Count it all joy, my brothers, when you meet trials of various kinds,*
*for you know that the testing of your faith produces steadfastness.*
*And let steadfastness have its full effect,*
*that you may be perfect and complete, lacking in nothing.*

James 1:2-4

God works tenaciously to conform us to the image of His Son. That's why He saves us. All the lessons we learn in life…the struggles we endure and trials we face…Jesus has promised to finish the work He started in us and work everything together for our good. All we have to do is cooperate with Him.

Jesus wastes nothing and uses everything. Sometimes life seems easy. Sometimes it can be hard. But regardless of what's going on in our lives…anxiety is not the answer. We are told to count it all joy when we fall into various trials knowing that Jesus has a plan and is in control.

## WEEK FIFTY

SATURDAY/SUNDAY *Learn and Grow*

Facts of Life:

-You were saved to know, love and enjoy God.

-It's up to you to take good care of your soul.

-We have everything we need to love as Jesus loves.

Personal Reflections:

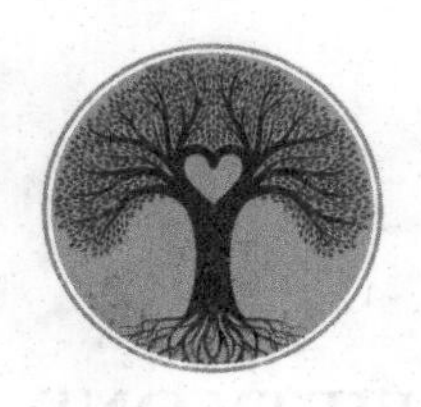

# WEEK FIFTY ONE

MONDAY *Abundance*

*I am the door. If anyone enters by me,*
*he will be saved and will go in and out and find pasture.*
*The thief comes only to steal and kill and destroy.*
*I came that they may have life and have it abundantly.*

John 10:9-10

Believing in Jesus is the only way to be *saved* from sin and receive the gift of a new, better and eternal life. "Only Jesus is the one true source for the knowledge of God and the basis for spiritual security." (John Mac Arthur)

Jesus saves us *from* hell *for* abundance. We're not talking about "abundance" in the worldly sense: popularity, fortune and fame and that sort of thing. We're talking about spiritual abundance… knowing Jesus intimately…the divine riches of heaven placed at our disposal and every good and perfect blessing that pertains to life and godliness. That is the kind of abundance that matters most.

# WEEK FIFTY ONE

TUESDAY *Abundance*

*Now to him who is able to do far more abundantly*
*than all that we ask or think, according*
*to the power at work within us,*
*to him be glory in the church and in Christ Jesus*
*throughout all generations, forever and ever. Amen.*

Ephesians 3:20-21

---

Living an abundant life is all about focusing on what Jesus can do, not obsessing over what we cannot do. Everything God says about Himself in scripture is true. All we have to do is believe Him. When He says He created something from nothing – He did. When He says He delivered two million people from captivity - He did. When He says He healed the sick and raised Himself from the grave – He did. And what He did back in Biblical times…He can still do. In fact He wants to.

God never changes. He is the same yesterday, today and forever. He doesn't lie. Why would He?

## WEEK FIFTY ONE

WEDNESDAY *Abundance*

*We want you to know, brothers, about the grace of God that has been given among the churches of Macedonia, for in a severe test of affliction, their abundance of joy and their extreme poverty have overflowed in a wealth of generosity on their part.*

II Corinthians 8:1-2

---

Earthly circumstances don't have to control our lives. There's a much better way to live. Besides - God wants more for us. But He lets us chose how we will live our lives. We can be victims or victors. We can live the abundant life Christ died to give us or succumb to the spiritual oppression that threatens to take us captive. We can fix our eyes on Jesus or...well, you get the idea.

Jesus doesn't save us so we can be oppressed by life. He's our Shepherd and longs to empower us and guide us and provide for us so that we will lack no good thing.

## WEEK FIFTY ONE

THURSDAY *Abundance*

*But you, O Lord, are a God merciful and gracious,*
*slow to anger and abounding in steadfast love and faithfulness.*

Psalm 86:15

---

God loves. He loves everyone. And it is His love, mercy and grace that enables us to succeed at living life. Surrender is the one thing He requires. Rebelling against God gets us nowhere. In fact, defying God only blocks the flow of His grace, which is the very thing we need to truly prosper and succeed for His glory. If we lack peace, power and joy in our lives it's not God's fault. He graciously gave us all those things and will bless us more and more, every day if we obey Him. We do not have to go without.

# WEEK FIFTY ONE

FRIDAY

*Abundance*

*His divine power has granted to us all things*
*that pertain to life and godliness,*
*through the knowledge of him who called*
*us to his own glory and excellence,*
*by which he has granted to us his precious and very great promises,*
*so that through them you may become*
*partakers of the divine nature,*
*having escaped from the corruption that is in*
*the world because of sinful desire.*
*For this very reason, make every effort to*
*supplement your faith with virtue,*
*and virtue with knowledge,*

II Peter 1:3-5

---

Christians are the wealthiest people on earth. The riches we possess are spiritual in nature, eternal and unchanging. They will not fade away with the passing of time and their value does not fluctuate like the stock market. Jesus has given us everything that pertains to living a successful God-honoring life. He didn't die just to save us *from* hell. He sacrificed His life to bless us with an extraordinary life. Hallelujah! What a Savior. Thank Him, every day. We owe Him everything.

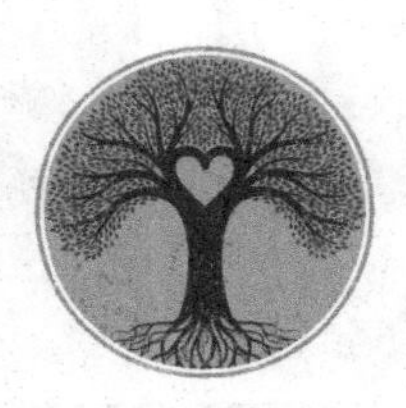

## WEEK FIFTY ONE

SATURDAY/SUNDAY 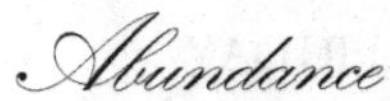

Facts of Life:

-God wants to fill you with the fullness of Himself.

-Jesus saved you for abundance.

-Knowing God is abundance.

Personal Reflections:

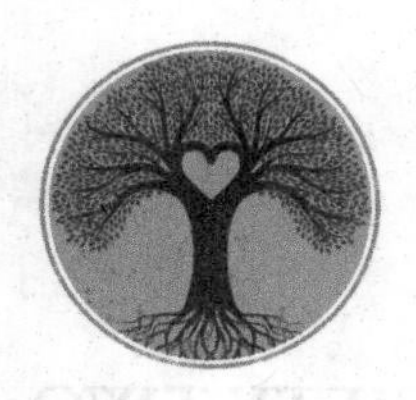

# WEEK FIFTY TWO

MONDAY

*Truth*

*But you, O Lord, are a God merciful and gracious,*
*slow to anger and abounding in steadfast love and faithfulness.*

Psalm 86:15

---

The definition of truth is: *That which is real, accurate and right.* The Bible says that God is not a man that He should lie. He tells us the truth and He tells us the truth about everything. We can trust Him. He cannot lie. He's God. It's important that we understand that all-important element in His nature.

The world is overflowing with unsubstantiated theories, philosophies, concepts and frail people who lie like you and me. That's one of the reasons why living on planet earth can be confusing and overwhelming at times. Putting our trust in Jesus is liberating. He tells us the truth. Allelujah. Amen.

# WEEK FIFTY TWO

TUESDAY *Truth*

*I am the way, and the truth, and the life.*
*No one comes to the Father except through me*

John 14:6

---

The truth we need to know about life, death, heaven, hell and salvation is found in God's Word. Jesus came to earth, lived, died for our sin and was buried. He raised Himself from the grave and is now in heaven seated at the right hand of His Father (I Corinthians 15:3-4).

The decision we make regarding Jesus will not only determine where we spend eternity but, also, how we will live our everyday lives. The truth about God's saving grace is available to everyone. Will we accept and embrace the "truth" about Jesus or reject it?

## WEEK FIFTY TWO

WEDNESDAY *Truth*

*You will know the truth, and the truth will set you free.*

John 8:32

---

Divine truth sets us free. I'm not just talking about setting us free from the power of sin and spending eternity in hell. I'm talking about the power of God's Word which sets us free from: hate, fear, addiction, self-absorption and anything and everything else that can hold the human spirit captive.

Jesus is willing to speak truth into our lives. But we have to listen. We were created and are saved to listen and obey God. That is the best possible way to live life.

# WEEK FIFTY TWO

THURSDAY *Truth*

*Have nothing to do with foolish, ignorant controversies;*
*you know that they breed quarrels.*
*And the Lord's servant must not be*
*quarrelsome but kind to everyone,*
*able to teach, patiently enduring evil.*

II Timothy 2:23-24

---

There is a diversity of thought and opinion in this ol' world. And yes, everyone does have the right to their own opinion. But according to God we're not supposed to argue about it. Instead, we're supposed to know His truth and speak His truth out loud, to others, in a loving, kind and gentle, non-judgmental way.

God's truth is the only thing that will correct what is wrong in our world and improve our lot in life. It's not about being right. It's about pointing others to Jesus Christ and telling the world about Him.

# WEEK FIFTY TWO

FRIDAY

*Truth*

*The sum of your word is truth,*
*and every one of your righteous rules endures forever.*

Psalm 119:160

---

The Bible is not half-truth and half lies. God's Word is one hundred percent true from beginning to end, Genesis through Revelation. Every book, chapter, and verse is God-breathed and inspired. Period! End of story.

There is a loving and perfect Someone who will tell us the truth and that we can believe in. His name is Jesus and we can trust Him. He gladly replaces the wrongness of our thinking with His divine light of truth. Talk about hope.

## WEEK FIFTY TWO

SATURDAY/SUNDAY

| Facts of Life: |
|---|
| -God tells us the truth about everything. |
| -God's truth sets us free. |
| -In God's Word we find hope. |

Personal Reflections: